Praise for *Get Out the*

"This book stands out as a distinctive, real-life story of reinvention. The hardest action to take is the initial one—and David Hollingsworth's insight and inspiration will guide you from the first step out the door into your personal sprint to success."

> — Scott McKain, CSP, CPAE, author, *Iconic*
> scottmckain.com

"Everyone loves a great comeback story, and David's will inspire you to take the first step towards yours!"

> — Eric Gelber, endurance athlete, featured in the Tribeca Film & Resonant
> Pictures documentary *200 Miles*
> www.tribecafilm.com/studios/200-miles

"The life lessons in this book are not secret formulas or quick fixes. They are a model for the amount of heart it takes to cross any finish line when the odds are not in your favor. Gift this book to someone who's having trouble with that first step out the door!"

> — David Goad, professional speaker and coach
> www.davidgoadspeaks.com

"Happiness is a life-long journey of learning how to use every fall as a chance to bounce, to go for what we want on every front, and live our lives full-out. In *Get Out the Door!*, David shows that once you take the first step, you're on your way."

> — Gopi Kallayil, Chief Evangelist, Brand Marketing at Google, author, *The
> Internet to the Inner-net and The Happy Human*
> kallayil.com

"David tells an exciting, real-life story that takes the reader from tragedy to triumph with humor and insight. *Get Out the Door!* will resonate with anyone who has had a personal setback or goal that seemed out of reach. The secret is in taking that first step by reading this book."

> — Doug Stevenson, CSP, author, *The Story Theater Method*
> www.storytelling-in-business.com

"David's story about overcoming a tragic accident through humor and hope shows that laughter can be mined from any subject. *Get Out the Door* is just what this country needs right now."

> — Greg Schwem, comedian and author of *The Road to Success Goes Through the Salad Bar*
> www.gregschwem.com

"*Get Out The Door!* is more than David Hollingsworth's story. It's your story, and mine, and everyone else's who comes up against life, which we all do. For me, the big takeaway is to take the first step, and that there will always be more first steps. David reminds me that I don't have to see the end in order to succeed. I just have to see that next mailbox. Read the book, and you'll know what I mean."

> — Joe Calloway, author, *The Leadership Mindset*
> www.joecalloway.com

"The trials of life constantly thwart our efforts to reach our ultimate destination. In *Get Out the Door!*, David Hollingsworth proves that even though life happens, once we take the first step, we can get there, and the rest is easy."

> — Mark L Brown, Certified Speaking Professional, World Champion of Public Speaking
> www.markbrownspeaks.com

"We have choices every day. You don't have to finish a marathon. You don't have to climb the steps of the Empire State Building. You DO have to make a choice. Make the right one. Read this book and be inspired to achieve more than you ever have before. Now, Get Out the Door and take that first step. You'll be glad you did."

— Comedian Rik Roberts
www.RikRoberts.com

Foreword By Bestselling Author Judy Carter

GET OUT THE DOOR!

How To Overcome Obstacles On The Road To High Performance

David Hollingsworth

INDIE BOOKS
INTERNATIONAL®

ISBN 13: 13: 978-1-952233-41-8
Library of Congress Control Number: 2021900819

Designed by Joni McPherson, mcphersongraphics.com

INDIE BOOKS INTERNATIONAL, INC. *
2424 VISTA WAY, SUITE 316
OCEANSIDE, CA 92054

www.indiebooksintl.com

For Binks

CONTENTS

FOREWORD

What makes a good story? One that is real and personal—that gets under people's skin and takes them on an emotional journey that truly inspires change and transformation.

When I wrote *The Message of You* in 2013, I knew its lessons were valuable for those who were looking for a way to tell their story. I had no idea it was going to touch so many people in different ways.

The key lesson from my book is that when you tell your story, others can see themselves in it, and if you tell it well, readers will identify with your story and apply your lessons to their lives. Telling your story can transform not only your life but also the lives of those around you. Your story reaches others in the advice you give to your friends, in the lessons you teach your children, in the stories you tell your family.

When I read my students' stories, I'm amazed at all the experience and insight they bring, and David's story is no different. When he started his journey, he had no idea where it would lead, but it's brought some interesting discoveries along the way. He learned how to transform his story, with all its twists and turns, from a mess into a message that entertains and inspires. That's what David has done here. He read my book, joined my group, and applied my lessons to his story. That's the life-transforming power of *The Message of You*.

In his story, David shows that the toughest part of achieving any goal or overcoming any obstacle isn't the journey or struggle—it's taking that first step. Once you get started, it can lead to all sorts of wonderful and amazing changes that come from the struggle and the growth you experience along the way. There is one thing you can do to make your life better tomorrow than it is today. There is one thing you can do consistently to achieve your goals and go where you want to go. Get started—it may be scary, but once you take the first step, you build momentum that carries you toward what you really want.

Or, as David says, "Get out the door. Once you do, the rest is easy." I'm excited about what you're about to learn, and even more excited to hear what changes you make in your life as you take those lessons to heart.

Judy Carter

Author, *The Message of You,*
The Comedy Bible, Stand Up Comedy:
The Book, and *The New Comedy Bible*

www.judycarter.com

PREFACE

This book is about how you can overcome any obstacle on your road to high performance. I know about that rocky road. This is a real-life comeback story.

Where do you want to go? Do you have big dreams that seem overwhelming when you try to turn them into action? Do you have trouble seeing yourself achieving what you've always wanted? Maybe you're looking for some secret formula that will put you on track toward your goals, some powerful technique that guarantees your success. Perhaps you're looking for a muse to inspire you to bigger and better accomplishments.

Here is the roadmap that will help you:

MILEPOSTS ON THE ROAD TO HIGH PERFORMANCE

Identify The Obstacle. Life happens to all of us. We have obstacles that prevent us from getting to where we want to go. To move forward, we have to identify the obstacle that's in our way. Until we do, we will stay stuck where we are.

Start With A Single Step. The longest journey begins with a single step. We have all heard that, but it is true. No matter how short or long that path is, you've got to take the first step to get there.

Commit To Change. Too many people stay stuck where they are because they are too scared, too scarred, or too secure in their current circumstances to risk making a change. To move forward, you have to accept what it will take to change and commit to making things different. To make them better.

Get Out The Door! The hardest part of any improvement effort is not the journey, the learning, or the growing; the hardest part is getting out there every day to go a little bit further, a little bit faster, or a little bit better. Once you get out the door, the rest is easy.

I've never thought of myself as an athlete, and to look at me, you might not think so, either. In 2012, I was fifty-one years old, eighty pounds overweight, depressed, and dealing with a ton of personal challenges.

By Thanksgiving 2012, I was sick and tired of being sick and tired. I knew I needed to change my eating habits but lacked motivation. I stepped onto the scale, and it hit 250.5 pounds. At 5'9" (on a good day), my weight was way over a healthy limit. I decided I needed to make some changes.

In 2014, I went from being a complete couch potato to achieving several racing goals that just a few years earlier would have seemed impossible.

My completion of a ten-year journey was not about winning races. I never won a race. In fact, I never finished anywhere near the front. Even though the triathlon swims were short, my arms and legs flailed so wildly that the race staff asked if I needed assistance. Watching me in a swim event was the same as throwing a cat into the pool. There was a lot of activity but little forward progress.

However, in the end, I finished every race I started. I anticipated the completion of these goals for a long time. When I share how far that journey took me, you may think I had some long-term goal-setting strategy or coaching that helped keep me focused.

The truth is, I didn't. I knew where I wanted to end up, but in the beginning, it was just an idea or seemed like a silly daydream. I had no idea how I was going to accomplish one or all of my goals. The exciting thing is, I never set out to run a marathon. I just kept doing something every day that eventually got me to where I wanted to go.

The fact of the matter is that there are very few secrets on the road to getting what you want. If someone claims they've found the secret and wants you to pay for it, you're likely to be disappointed and have a bit less money in your pocket. That's right. There are no secrets. If you're looking for those, I'd put this down right now, and look for a different book in the philosophy or fiction section.

However, there are some revelations I've discovered, some lessons I've learned—many the hard way—and a journey with more dips, twists, turns, and drops than many roller coasters.

My journey may be unique to me, but I believe our stories are very similar, and we all want to go to places we've never been. We all want to achieve things when others may doubt our ability or commitment. We all run into obstacles or setbacks that make us wonder if the goal is worth it.

I'll tell you upfront. The path to your goals is rarely a straight line. It's full of obstacles, naysayers, left turns, and self-doubt. It was hard for me to stay focused on the big goal when everyday life kept throwing little things at me that tried to knock me off balance. I was never consistent about writing down my goals, throwing myself into my workouts, eating perfectly, or leveraging others' experience.

The one thing I did, consistently, was: get out the door! After that, the rest was easy.

This book is about getting started on the road to high performance. If you decide to stop reading and move on, you will miss out on what happens next—or really—what happened first that put me in the condition I've just described.

You will also miss out on how to take what I've learned and apply it to your own circumstances, far surpassing anything I did. I'd hate for you to stop here and miss out on learning from my mistakes and setbacks.

If you've got even average ability and determination, you're way ahead of me. So, let's get started.

David Hollingsworth
Washington, DC, 2020

PART ONE

IDENTIFY THE OBSTACLE

WHAT JUST HAPPENED?

*"You've been in an accident.
We're taking you to the hospital."*

I opened my eyes and tried to make sense of what just happened. I could see clouds and eventually figured out I was looking up toward the sky. The air was so thick and muggy that it was hard to breathe, and underneath, it felt like I was being cooked in a skillet. I could not hear well. My head was weighed down and seemed like it was inside a giant pillow. It took me a few minutes to understand that someone was talking loudly and a bit longer to figure out he was asking questions.

"Are you all right?"

"Are you okay?"

My eyes finally focused on a face looking down at me. Even though he tried to sound confident and reassuring, I could see the look of worry in his eyes. I had no idea who he was, where I was, or how I got there. All I knew was that someone was looking down at me, yelling and telling me not to move. Nearby, I could hear a small engine sputtering along.

While I was held down, I attempted to assess what was going on, but nothing seemed to make sense. It was hot outside, but I felt like I was overdressed. I had on long pants, a jacket, gloves, and something keeping my head and face warm. I was hot, sweaty, and covered from head to toe in gear that felt out of place for the middle of July.

As I tried to figure things out, I started to do an inventory of what I could do without getting yelled at by the person who was talking to me. I could move my eyes back and forth. I could wiggle my fingers. I worked my way down, flexing and relaxing muscles to see if I could tell what was going on. My legs seemed like they were being held down, so I didn't try to move them. I tried to wiggle my toes. My left toes seemed to work just fine, but when I tried to wiggle my right toes, I was interrupted by what seemed to be some voices getting louder.

As the voices got closer, I could tell there were several people, but because they sounded muffled, I could not make out what they were saying. I heard snippets of something like, "Who is that?" and "Is he going to be okay?" The hot surface underneath me became identifiable as asphalt, but I didn't know why I'd willingly lie on my back in a parking lot. At that point, I could hear a siren getting louder and louder. I heard a large truck pull into the lot, with doors opening and closing.

The face I'd looked up to was replaced by a couple of different faces. These faces looked just as serious but much more businesslike. Both people were wearing identical shirts, with a flag on one sleeve and a patch on the other that said, "FIRE & RESCUE DEPARTMENT." One kept looking at my face while talking to me, as the other started looking up and down my body and started feeling body parts with gloved hands. I wondered what he was trying to do with all the poking and prodding.

The first questions were replaced by a new set of questions.

"Do you remember what happened?"

"Tell me where you hurt."

"Do you have any allergies?"

"Have you taken any medications?"

"Do you have any medical history we should know about?"

"Is there anyone we should call?"

I mumbled some replies, not sure what I was saying. Neither the questions nor answers seemed to make any sense, at least compared to what I wanted to ask, like, "Who are you?" or "How did I get here?" I wanted to get up and see what was happening around me, but a pair of hands held me down, preventing me from moving. I couldn't turn my head or see what was going on. The duo continued to work in an efficient manner, poking, prodding, and relaying numbers to each other as they recorded the information.

I tried to answer as best I could, but it was still hard to hear, and it was difficult to move my head or open my mouth. I could feel them taking my pulse and checking to see if I had any broken bones or bleeding. A pair of gloved hands fumbled under my chin, pushing and pulling on something. When I felt them pull away, I could breathe a bit easier, but I didn't know why my head felt so heavy. I took some comfort in realizing that all my teeth seemed to be intact.

The duo made a couple more checks, noted their findings, and strapped me to a board of some kind. For some reason, I didn't seem to be wearing any shoes. Starting with my ankles, they strapped my legs down so I could not move them at all. Next, they strapped my hips down, then my chest, then each arm. I could wiggle my fingers, but with the straps, I could not move anything else.

At this point, I hurt all over, but being strapped down, it didn't hurt when I moved because it was impossible to move from my neck down. One person put what felt like a plastic brace on my neck, while the other strapped down my head. I realized why I couldn't feel the strap on my head was because I was wearing a helmet, which explained why my head felt heavy, and it was hard to hear. I was strapped down so tightly, and I couldn't turn my head left or right. All I could do was look up and try to catch things in my peripheral vision.

As I was loaded into the back of the ambulance, out of the corner of my eye, through the small crowd, I recognized the parking lot of a local elementary school. I saw a number of people whose faces reflected a sense of being worried. A few of them relayed information to others on their phones. When I glanced to the other side, I saw a pair of boots; some broken glass; a helmet; and a pile of twisted plastic, rubber, and metal that my brain eventually recognized as my motorcycle. The front wheel was bent but still turning when someone reached down and shut off the engine.

I was buckled into the back of the ambulance. One person climbed in with me, and the other climbed into the front of the vehicle. The doors slammed shut, the truck rumbled to life, and the siren wailed. I asked the attendant, "What happened?"

"You've been in an accident. We're taking you to the hospital."

2

MIDLIFE CRISIS

*When I turned 40, the itch to ride
a motorcycle started to come back.*

When I was in my early forties, I was probably in the midst of what you might call a midlife crisis. Lots of people go through a phase where they're bored, in a rut, or want to try things they haven't done before. I've always loved to try new things, and usually, the faster, the better.

When I was a kid, I had a big fear of heights. I didn't like going on Ferris wheels, roller coasters, or bridges. I didn't even like going up inside of a tall building, let alone stand on the roof. Over time, I learned how to deal with that fear and discovered I *liked* roller coasters. Sure, they were scary, and there was a lot of tension as we'd start climbing, but once the coaster got to the top of that first hill and screamed down the other side, I was joyfully screaming along with the other riders.

Did I say I like roller coasters? I *love* roller coasters. The bigger, steeper, and faster they are, the better. I've ridden a variety of roller coasters from the older, traditional wooden ones to the most modern steel coasters. Looping coasters? *Been there.* Standing coaster? *Done that.* Vertical climb, ninety-degree descent, launch coasters? *Awesome.* I've even ridden Top Thrill Dragster at Cedar Point in Ohio and Kingda Ka at Six Flags Great America in New Jersey, where you are launched from zero to 120 mph in less than four seconds, shot straight up 400 feet, then back down the other side.

When I go on that teacup ride at Disney World, I'm done for the day. I can go fast, but I don't spin well.

When I was a kid, I had a fascination with motorcycles. My mom was adamant that I didn't get on one. Since my uncle was involved in a motorcycle accident, she felt she didn't need to harp on the issue. I agreed. I did not want to be in an accident and made it through high school and college without getting on a motorcycle.

When I got married, I still played it safe. I met Maggie[1] when I lived in Connecticut back in the late 1980s. We were both active and liked a lot of the same things, even if we came from different backgrounds. I grew up in a blue-collar Midwest family, and Maggie was an Ivy-Leaguer from the East Coast. We moved to the Washington, DC, area in the early 1990s, got married, and started a family.

With our two kids, Jamie and Lauren, we had our hands full, but that was fine with me. We shared all the duties involved in running a household, as well as the fun parts of raising a young family. We juggled the family responsibilities along with taking time to enjoy fun things in the DC area and around the country with our children.

---

[1] Some names have been changed for privacy.

As the kids got into school, we started to have a bit more time for personal pursuits. Up until that point, I had never considered learning how to ride a motorcycle, but I wondered if it was a hobby I wanted to pursue.

When I turned forty, the itch to ride a motorcycle started to come back. I was involved in autocross and other racing events and felt I could handle learning how to ride a motorcycle. Lots of my friends were getting bikes, and I wanted one, too. I started researching how to pick a motorcycle, the best methods for learning how to ride, and what safety equipment to buy. One day, I got my motorcycle. It wasn't some big Harley Davidson V-twin like all of my friends had. It was a little Honda Rebel 250—the quintessential entry-level bike. I found a slightly used one that had literally been driven by a little old lady on weekends. I figured if she could handle it, I could. I bought a full-face helmet, armored riding jacket, riding boots, gloves, and heavy jeans to complete my outfit. I assured everyone I was going to be smart about learning how to ride. I was the perfect illustration of born to be mild.

My midlife crisis machine: Honda Rebel 250.

Mild suited me well because I knew what I did could affect Maggie and the kids. I didn't want to do anything so risky that it might impact them negatively. I'd watch videos for beginning riders; familiarize myself with all the motorcycle controls; and practice riding around the neighborhood, away from traffic, and only at times when cars weren't likely to be around. I got my provisional motorcycle license from the Department of Motor Vehicles (DMV) and signed up for a Motorcycle Safety Foundation class to make sure I learned to ride safely.

I went about my midlife crisis in a relatively sensible and logical fashion. I've always had a fascination for learning new things, and this seemed like an opportunity to test that theory. I subscribed to motorcycle forums, bought magazines, and hung out at the motorcycle shop. There were young riders wanting the fastest, most exotic sportbike legally possible. The old grizzled riders who turned their noses up at any bike that wasn't built in the US had a presence. And what about those boomer and Generation-X riders who finally had enough disposable income to buy whatever they wanted? At least they could look the part of being a motorcycle rider, even if their wallets were a lot thicker than their skill and experience. Anyone can be a motorcycle enthusiast.

I just wanted to be a normal, average rider. I had no desire to go too fast, no need to impress other people, and no penchant for loud pipes or stunt riding. I just wanted to learn so I could occasionally enjoy a ride to work in good weather or go for rides in the mountains and enjoy the scenery. Probably the most boring midlife crisis you could imagine was good enough for me.

Over the early spring and summer, I'd get home from work, spend time with Maggie and the kids, walk the dog, and then suit up to get some riding in. I'd check the brakes and throttle, make sure there were no loose parts or worry spots on the bike. I checked my gear to make sure my jacket and helmet fit well, and I had good visibility on the streets. I'd get on the bike, make a few imaginary revs, and start it up. My smaller bike was not loud, but it was good enough for me.

I enjoyed riding around the block, taking the bike to the store instead of driving a car, and liked life on two wheels. I'd always loved riding bicycles, but this was different. I could sit at a stop sign and make the bike go "run-na-na-na-na," and get away from traffic at a light just by pushing the throttle a bit. I didn't have to go fast, but I could go fast enough.

I was aware there were lots of things that could hurt me. Even though I rode a red bike and wore a white helmet and lots of reflective bits, I was still invisible to cars. That is probably a motorcycle rider's biggest fear—that cars, trucks, and SUVs don't see you. I was hypervigilant of vehicles and let them have the right of way every time. Because if we hit each other, they might have a dent, but my body is a little harder to repair than a fender. I ensured I gave cars plenty of leeway, as well as pedestrians, bicyclists, and anyone else out there.

I quickly learned to be a safe rider as I attempted to be aware of all the potential hazards. To paraphrase Robert Burns, "The best-laid schemes o' mice an' men (and motorcycle riders) gang aft agley."

When I set out for a quick ride on July 9, 2004, I had no idea just how far "agley" those best-laid plans were about to go.

3

HITTING THE WALL

Things happened so quickly that
I didn't have time to react.

I spent my spare time riding my little Honda motorcycle around the neighborhood throughout the spring and early summer of 2004. I knew Maggie was nervous about the motorcycle, and I wanted to make sure she knew I was practicing safe skills.

I signed up for a Motorcycle Safety Foundation (MSF) Basic Rider Course. MSF offers classes in beginner through advanced riding skills. My class was a couple of months away, so I researched as much as I could, limited my riding to the neighborhood, and practiced my skills in the local elementary school parking lot.

Slowly but surely, I got a little more confident in keeping the bike upright, starting, stopping, and turning. I felt like it was going well and looked forward to making my status official by qualifying for my motorcycle endorsement. I talked to some friends with sportbikes who gave me a hard time for "just riding a Honda Rebel 250," but that didn't bother me much. I was happy just to be learning.

One beautiful summer day, the sun was shining without the typical Washington DC humidity, making it a perfect day to ride. Maggie was with her parents in North Carolina. I got home just as the nanny departed for a Sting concert. It was also my mom's birthday. The kids (ages six and nine) were preoccupied with a video and didn't notice that I came home.

I reasoned I had just enough time to take the bike for a practice spin around the block and was only going to be gone for a few minutes. When I got back, we'd all get dinner. I put on all my gear, started up the bike, and headed toward the empty Oak Hill Elementary parking lot. It was a perfect Friday afternoon because everyone had gone home for the day.

I turned the key, started the motorcycle with just one kick, slowly backed it out of the garage, turned around in the driveway, and rolled out into the street, giving the kids a little salute through the window as I headed toward the school parking lot. Once I got to the school, I rode around the lot a few times. I practiced some starts and stops, S-turns, and a couple of acceleration runs before going back to figure-eights and working on right and left turns.

I revved the engine at one end and took off across the parking lot. Looking back, it was irresponsible. While I'm sure lots of parents have plopped their kids in front of a video to run to the store, and while the kids knew to go next door in an emergency, six and nine are pretty young ages. I assumed everything was okay to run out because I was sure I was going to be right back.

At the school, I wanted to work on some stops. I'd accelerate across the lot and brake hard to stop quickly, just in case I had to in real traffic. Partway through, I hit a patch of sand and started to lose my balance. When I felt that happening, I gripped the handlebar, which also happened to be on the throttle. I instinctively grabbed and gripped it hard. I shot forward as the bike accelerated across the parking lot. Things happened so quickly that I didn't have time to react. Instead of letting go of the throttle or hitting the brakes, I headed right for the edge of the lot.

If I'd hit one foot to the right or left, I'd have bounced on the curb, over the handlebars, and into the grass. I'd have been embarrassed, and maybe a little scratched up, with some wounded pride to boot.

As the bike screamed across the parking lot, I froze. It seemed to take forever, but it was just a second or two. I headed for the end of the parking lot; my eyes locked in on the tree just beyond the curb. My mouth dry and heart racing, I didn't seem to be able to hit the clutch or brake and kept gaining speed. Before I could react, the bike hit the curb, coming to a dead stop.

When that happened, I was launched into the air, and my body continued to travel at the same speed. I bounced up off the bike, came down, and hit the edge of the curb so hard I could feel the air being knocked out of me.

I came to rest on the pavement. The bike came to rest against a nearby tree with the front wheel still spinning. As I heard the engine sputtering, I wanted to swear, but I could barely speak after the hit. All I knew was that it hurt—a lot—but I couldn't figure out precisely what hurt.

I reached one hand toward my helmet to lift my visor and assess what had happened, then dropped my head.

And things went black.

4

SHATTERED

*At this point, I was pretty
overwhelmed. I knew the injury was bad.*

The ambulance had a strange smell, like a combination of antiseptic and diesel fumes. The driver was careful not to make any sudden moves. I couldn't see where we were going, so I tried to guess where we were by the number of turns we made.

Even though I was strapped to a board, my mind raced.

The kids are at home by themselves, the nanny is out, and Maggie is hundreds of miles away!

Why can't I feel my right leg? Will I ever be able to move again?

"Is there anyone we can call?"

"A doctor would be nice about now."

"Seriously—who can we call?"

"Yes, my kids are at home alone. Please call my neighbor."

He dialed the number, held the bulky handset up to my helmet, and turned on the speakerphone.

"Heidi, this is David. I've been in an accident, and they're taking me to the ER to get checked out. The kids are home alone, and I'm on my way to the hospital. Will you please get to the house, call Maggie, and let her know I will call her when I can?"

"Oh my God, Dave! Are you going to be all right?"

"I have to go. Please keep the kids calm. I don't want them to panic. I will call them as soon as possible."

The paramedic took the phone back so I would not turn, twist, or do anything that might further injure myself. At least the kids were okay now.

As we drove toward the hospital, I wondered how bad the injury might be, and what might be ahead of me. Even though the driver cautiously avoided bumps, I could feel every hairline crack or bump in the pavement, sending a shock wave of pain up my back and down my left leg. I could hear them talking about a fractured vertebra, degraded sensation, as well as other words I may or may not have understood, but their tone of voice let me know it was serious. They were talking to the hospital as they drove to let them know there was a significant trauma case on its way.

The ambulance pulled up to the hospital and slowed to a stop. The paramedics carefully removed my stretcher from the vehicle and wheeled me into the Emergency Room. I haven't been to the ER that often, but I knew this time, I'd be going straight to the front of the line.

I noticed something else while I was on the stretcher. ER staff have one job—to assess, prioritize, and treat patients as best they can, quickly and professionally. From my experience, they do an amazing job. That doesn't mean they're gentle about it. They need to determine the seriousness of any injury and make sure you're getting the right treatment quickly, so nurses, technicians, and doctors talk slowly and loudly.

"Mr. Hollingsworth, look into the light."

"What day is it?"

"Friday, I think."

"Can you wiggle your fingers or toes?"

"I'm trying, okay?"

"Wake up! You can't go to sleep!"

"Dammit, I'm doing the best I can!"

The interrogation went on for what felt like forever. It was a barrage of constant questions, with lots of repeating, either because I didn't answer or gave different answers.

"When did you eat or drink last?"

"I think it was lunchtime."

"Have you had any alcohol?"

"No, have you got any?"

"Who is your next of kin?"

"Geez, how bad is it?"

I answered as best as I could, and I had vague recollections of people mentioning that they had Maggie on the phone, or they were talking to the neighbors and that the kids were okay. I was not allowed to talk on the phone, and I could feel all sorts of invasive tests and procedures. At some point, my helmet was removed, but I don't remember who took it off. I was prepped for an x-ray, and a couple of orderlies came to wheel me down the hall for the first internal look at what the damage might be. The pain was pretty intense, but I hadn't had any medication yet. I thought I'd like to get some, though. Soon.

At this point, I was pretty overwhelmed. I knew the injury was bad. I had no idea if Maggie or the kids knew the extent of what was going on, and I wasn't even sure if anyone had told them how serious things were because I certainly didn't know, and I'm not sure if the doctors knew at that point, either. I lay there strapped to a board, getting wheeled from room to room for x-rays, CT scans, blood tests, IVs, and lots of masked faces looking down at me while I looked up, trying to figure out what was going on.

I lost all concept of time. I tracked my location by counting tiles on the ceiling, or how many doors I got wheeled through. It had only been a couple of hours, but it felt like days as more specialists showed up to see what they could figure out from looking at me or reviewing the test results.

I'm sure my answers became less coherent because, at some point, I closed my eyes and just passed out. When I woke up, I'd been moved to a room near the main ER. It must have been a full twenty-four hours later because my wife, Maggie, sat next to my bed. She'd driven back home from North Carolina as fast as she could.

I asked, "How are the kids?"

"They're okay." Maggie looked pretty shaken, and I could see that she was stressed and concerned. Heck, everybody I could see looked stressed and worried. The nurses did, the orderlies did, and even people passing by in the hallway got quiet as they walked by. I was told I'd need spinal surgery, and the doctor on duty was paged and would be there shortly.

It may seem like a long time when you sit in a typical waiting room. In the ER, waiting for anything seems like an eternity. I could hear the clock, tick-tick-ticking, and I had nothing I could do other than count its ticks, my breathing, or heartbeats, which, since I could count them, I took to be a good sign.

```
PREOPERATIVE DIAGNOSIS:
    1.  L2 burst fracture with incomplete neurologic injury.
    2.  Multiple dural tears (posttraumatic).

POSTOPERATIVE DIAGNOSIS:
    1.  L2 burst fracture with incomplete neurologic injury.
    2.  Multiple dural tears (posttraumatic).

OPERATION:
    1.  Open fracture treatment.
    2.  Laminectomy L1 and L2.
    3.  Arthrodesis T12 to L3.
    4.  Spinal instrumentation T12 to L3 (Moss Miami system).
    5.  Harvest of iliac crest bone graft, right iliac crest.
    6.  Repair of dural leak.
```

The initial report didn't look good.

Eventually, I heard a bunch of voices talking in the hallway, and the doctor entered the room. He held a clipboard, several reports, and what appeared to be a copy of my x-rays. The spinal surgeon, Dr. Childs, stepped up and gave me his assessment:

"You've been through a lot. You've got an explosive burst fracture of your L2 vertebrae on three axes. It's essentially been broken into a lot of pieces."

"You've got a 60 percent compression of the spinal canal, and we're going to have to take you into surgery."

"We'll do everything we can, but—"

"We don't know if you're going to walk again."

Wow. I knew this was bad, but now I had to think about how bad it might be. I had been in a lot of accidents growing up, with more than my share of bumps, bruises, stitches, and even broken bones, but never had any news as life-altering as this. I recalled that I was hit by a car at the age of six. My family pulled into church one Sunday, and before checking traffic, I burst out the car door and ran across the street, right into the path of an oncoming car. Fortunately, it wasn't going that fast. I took a corner bumper shot off my backside, popped up in the air, landed upright on the sidewalk, and took off running. I was not seriously hurt. The worst part was that my mom got to see that I was wearing holey underwear after we got to the hospital.

This accident was much more severe. I wondered what life might be like if I couldn't walk. Maggie asked Dr. Childs about the surgery. I tried to distract myself from thinking about the possibilities.

Dr. Childs picked up a spinal model from the table. "We're going to use a bone graft from your hip to give enough solid surface to glue your L2 vertebrae back together."

"You're going to glue me back together?"

"It's a bit more complicated than that, but it's a basic description of how we're going to start. In addition, we're going to perform a laminectomy to remove bone that may be pinching on nerves and a four-level spinal fusion, from T12 to L3."

"That sounds like a lot of work."

"We wouldn't do it if you didn't need it. You're in good hands here."

Because the surgery was going to be extensive, it took another two days to stabilize me before it could take place. By this point, even though I was on a completely liquid diet with no solid food, I had a catheter inserted and had to wear an adult diaper because I had little to no ability to control that function, and clearly couldn't get up and go to the bathroom. The only control I had was one button to provide a timed morphine drip and another to call the nurse.

I was prepped for surgery, given an anesthetic, and I was out. The surgery took over six hours. I took a long time to wake up out of the anesthesia in the recovery room. When I came to, I was fitted for a Thoracic Lumbar Sacral Orthosis (TLSO) brace. It was a big plastic clamshell with straps that held it, and me, together to keep my spine from moving. It went from my armpits all the way down to my hips.

Name at Time of Exam: HOLLINGSWORTH, DAVID

Final Report

Order Number: 90002
Date of Exam: Jul 10 2004 1:34AM

EXAMINATION: CT2-0217 CT LUMBAR SPINE WO CONTRAST

CLINICAL INDICATIONS: Lumbar spine fracture.

TECHNIQUE: Spiral CT scanning was performed with 5 mm collimation with image reconstruction at 3 mm intervals. The axial data was reformatted and reconstructed in the sagittal plane.

INTERPRETATION: Correlation is made with plain radiographs showing the presence of six lumbar vertebrae. Using this numbering, there is a comminuted fracture of the L3 vertebral body extending into the right pedicle. There is a large retropulsed fragment arising from the superior aspect of the body extending into the spinal canal. The fragment measures approximately 1.0 x 1.5 cm and narrows the AP diameter of the canal by approximately 50%. The fracture extends to involve the lamina on the right side and this fracture is displaced by approximately 5 mm. No other fractures are identified.

IMPRESSION: COMMINUTED FRACTURE INVOLVING THE L3 VERTEBRAL BODY AND THE RIGHT-SIDED PEDICLE. THERE IS A LARGE RETROPULSED FRAGMENT CAUSING SIGNIFICANT NARROWING OF THE SPINAL CANAL IN THE AP DIMENSION.

Once surgery was complete, it didn't look much better.

While it provided me stability, I felt like a turtle on its back, unable to do anything other than pushing the button for the nurse.

For the next ten days, I remained in the critical care unit at the hospital. The staff cared for my surgical incision; I was x-rayed, scanned, sampled, and studied. Post-surgery, I was still in a lot of pain. However, the feeling was coming back to my right leg. It was a lot weaker than the left, but my foot responded to being poked with a needle. I could wiggle my toes. While wearing the brace, I could raise my bed slightly to watch television, but going to the bathroom on my own was out of the question, so I was 100 percent dependent upon the nurses.

While the morphine helped with the pain, it didn't help with sleep. I was awake for about twenty hours every day, drifting off when I could no longer keep my eyes open. I tried to read a bit, but for the most part, I watched documentaries and classic movies on television. Over time, it got hard to tell the shows apart from each other from my lack of sleep. Even the movies seemed to blur into one another.

I had a few visitors during my critical care days. Maggie would come by daily, but she had to care for the children, which cut her visits short. By this time, I could tell she was pretty upset with me. Some neighbors came by to let me know they'd be helping with the kids as much as they could, too. I got to talk to my parents and siblings on the phone, and while I could report improvement with my right leg, I didn't know what the prognosis would be. Dr. Childs reassured me the improvement was a good sign, and things would keep getting better.

After ten days, the critical care team felt I was ready to go to a rehab hospital. Since the move was planned for a weekend, they wanted to see if I could stand or take any steps before the move. I felt pretty weak but agreed to try. The nurses helped steady me as they sat me upright and held a walker in front of me. I placed my hands on the rails, and with their help, started to push off the bed—and fell straight to the floor. I folded like a cheap lawn chair.

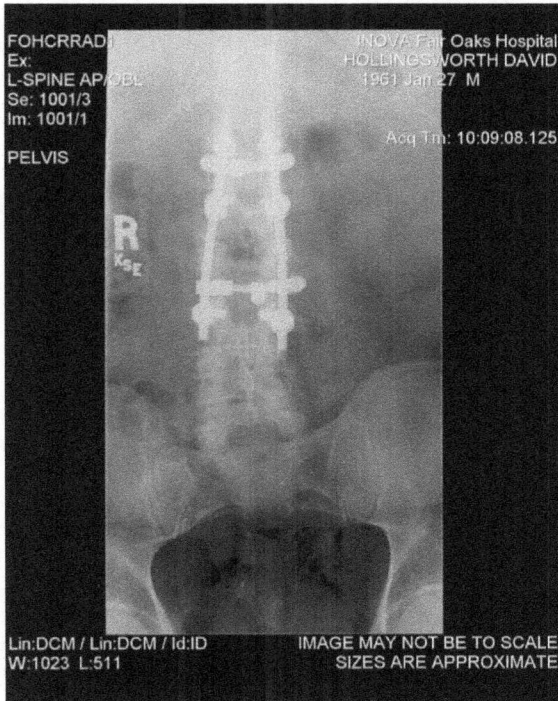

I was pretty much bolted back together.

While I had feeling in my right leg, I had zero strength. I could not support my own weight. The nurses helped me back into bed, and while there was a concern, the hospital needed the critical care bed, so I was slated for discharge the next morning. That verdict remained in place, even though the effort to stand and subsequent fall caused me to get nauseous and start vomiting the foulest substance I had ever seen or smelled. The impact from the fall had caused blood to pool in my stomach, which was now going to make its way back out through the shortest path possible.

I heard snippets of conversation: "I don't know if he's ready to go yet," "We've already got someone moved into his room," "The order is already set—he's got to go." There was lots of discussion about whether to reschedule the move, but the decision was final. I was being moved, whether I was ready or not.

5

ROUGH RIDE

"Hello, Mr. David. I am your new nurse. You can call me Peace."

The next morning, I woke up and saw the orderly pack my clothes and other items into a large bag. The on-duty nurse came in and said, "You're being transferred to Mount Vernon Rehabilitation Hospital in Alexandria."

I asked, "Isn't there anything closer?" While being in critical care was difficult, at least it was less than five miles from our home. The rehab hospital was at least a forty-five-minute drive away, so having visitors was going to be harder and take more time. All of my friends and co-workers lived nearby.

Around noon, the ambulance driver and another medical technician came into the room. "Are you ready to roll?"

I said, "Not really, but I don't think that makes a difference."

Critical care had done what they could do, the bed was valuable real estate, and the rehab hospital would be much better equipped to handle whatever came in this next stage.

Since I was in the TLSO brace, I didn't need to have my back immobilized, but was strapped to a stretcher and wheeled out to the ambulance waiting at the ER entrance. When I rolled through the hall, I felt like a kind of celebrity as people in the hallways parted in the middle. I counted the ceiling tiles as we turned corners. I took note of the changing smells as we rolled down the hall and wiggled my toes to see if they still worked. We eventually passed through the double doors from the inside of the ER to the main waiting area. I could get a glimpse of the people in the waiting room out of my side vision, and everyone there looked as if they didn't need to be there. At least I was moving on to a new location.

As I was wheeled out the doors to the waiting ambulance, I could smell fresh air mixed with diesel fumes. The ambulance was already running and right outside the door. The late summer air was so thick you could taste it, and the humidity stuck to me like water drops on a waxed car.

One attendant climbed up into the back of the ambulance and positioned the stretcher. The other steadied the opposite end as they slid me right into the back of the vehicle. They locked down the stretcher and closed the back doors. I could hear the footsteps of the driver as he walked around to the front of the ambulance to climb into the driver's seat. My attendant buckled in next to me to keep a watch during the trip. At first, things went smoothly. Familiar with the area, I could only estimate what route we might take, even though I could not see anything other than the interior of the ambulance.

The driver carefully avoided bumps or sudden turns. Every minor bump still sent a painful shockwave through my back and legs. It is a good thing I hadn't eaten any solid food for over a week since surgery because I started to feel a bit queasy.

I've never been a good passenger. If I have the choice between sitting in the passenger seat of a car and driving myself, I'll drive every time. When I'm a passenger, I must be careful that I don't try to read or do anything other than look straight ahead because I'm pretty susceptible to motion sickness. I can ride any roller coaster ever built, but put me on the teacup ride, and I'm done for the day.

At first, I thought the nausea would go away, but it didn't. It worsened. I told the attendant I was going to need a container because even though I hadn't eaten for a week, whatever was in my stomach was going to come up. And it did. The misery of my whole body reacting to the nausea, about twelve times, seemed worse than the accident. Every time, my ribs, back, and legs would send a searing pain all the way down to my toes.

When I've been sick before, throwing up once is usually enough to make me feel better, but each time now, I felt worse. I was finally getting rid of the residual gunk in my stomach from the initial impact. It was dark, sticky stuff, and while the attendant tried to make me feel like it was no big deal, the look on his face spoke volumes.

After about the fourth or fifth time I threw up, the attendant asked the driver, "Should we go back to Fair Oaks? He's not doing too well."

The driver said, "We're almost there. Let me get Mount Vernon on the line. They'll know if we should turn around and go back or keep going." My heart rate and blood pressure were high, and there was a concern, but the decision was made to keep going since the new hospital was expecting me, and turning around would put me right back in the ER.

I finally stopped vomiting and sipped some water. I was soaked in sweat, and my stomach muscles felt like I'd gone ten rounds with Mike Tyson. The ambulance slowed down. I sensed that the attendant was relieved the ride was almost over. I noticed we were finally off the highway, stopping at traffic lights and going over a few painful speed bumps, but I was not nearly in as much distress as the earlier part of the ride.

We pulled up to the Inova Mount Vernon Hospital, close to the Potomac River and near the home of George Washington. I couldn't tell it from the inside of the ambulance, because I was still looking at the ceiling. The vehicle stopped, and the driver came around to open the doors. The attendant unlatched my stretcher from the ambulance, and they worked together to get me down out of the vehicle. The receiving medical team was there to meet us, and the ambulance crew quickly handed me over, apparently relieved to be going home.

At the new hospital, I got to see a lot of new faces looking down at me as I was wheeled out of the sweltering summer sun and into the air-conditioned hospital. I counted doors, ceiling tiles, and elevators as I was moved from floor to floor. We eventually reached the rehabilitation receiving area. I waited for what seemed like forever. I didn't have any distractions like music or television to occupy my mind, so I tried to entertain myself by counting the number of holes in the ceiling tiles.

Finally, I heard the door open, clipboards and charts snap together, and a pen click rhythmically as someone new was in the room, even if I couldn't see who it was. After what seemed like an eternity of minor administrative tasks, I looked up to see a round face with brown skin and striking brown eyes look down at me.

"Hello, Mr. David. I am your new nurse. You can call me Peace."

6

BREATHE

*I felt an incredible amount of relief that
things were going to get better.*

Peace was my intake nurse at Mount Vernon Hospital. She was friendly but businesslike as she recorded my vital signs. She was competent but seemed stressed. I wasn't sure whether it was my condition or her heavy caseload. Most nurses I've met have had way too many patients and not enough time.

I noticed Peace had an accent. "Where are you from originally?"

Peace replied, "I'm from Ghana. I've been here for a few years, though."

Peace went back to her tests and paperwork, signed me into the rehabilitation hospital, and called to have me moved to a room while she went on to the next patient.

Since I was by myself, I tried to occupy my mind with whatever little distraction I could find. The television wasn't working, so I counted on my fingers and wiggled my toes to make sure my legs still worked. I was still a little woozy from the ambulance ride; I hoped that part was over. It wasn't. I began to feel queasy again and started to vomit again. I rang the emergency call button.

Peace ran in and called for the doctor on duty. I could hear them discussing what to do, and the topic of sending me back to the critical care hospital came up. I think it was a real possibility for a while, but then the doctor came in and said, "We're going to intubate you to clear that stuff out of your stomach—it seems like your body wants it out of there, and we're going to help it get out. It should make things easier once we're done."

I had no idea what intubate meant. I assumed it meant using a tube for something, and that's all I knew. I signed a document I didn't understand and quickly learned it was not a gentle procedure. A long plastic tube was inserted into my nose, and I gagged as it went down my throat and into my stomach. I felt like I was being suffocated because I could not breathe every time I closed my mouth. I attempted to keep my mouth slightly open to avoid gasping for air, even though I was constantly gasping for air.

I couldn't swallow at all and had difficulty breathing. Every time I closed my lips together, I felt like I was being smothered. I was unable to talk, but I could write notes. I wrote a note to ask for a bowl of water and a washcloth so I could keep my lips from getting too dry because of my open mouth. I watched the contents of my stomach going out through the tube, which didn't make me feel any better. Even with the tube in, I still vomited several times. Each time, Peace ran in to help me out. Eventually, I seemed to stabilize. The tube in my throat continued to make it almost impossible to breathe.

CHAPTER 6

As the night wore on, I struggled to fall asleep. I'd relax, and all of a sudden, find myself gasping for air. Each time, a nurse would run in to check on me. They were doing their job well, but each time I felt worse. Each time I found it harder to breathe, I'd get more anxious.

After fourteen hours with the tube in, I rang the call button. The duty nurse appeared and asked what was going on. I wrote on my pad and handed her the note. "Take this thing out."

"We can't do that. The doctor gave specific instructions, and I don't know what will happen."

I wrote, "I don't care."

And I didn't. I wanted to breathe, and with this tube in, I could not. It had been nearly two weeks of tests, surgery, poking and prodding, and being reduced to depending on other people for even the most basic bodily functions. I was angry, I was tired, and I was done. At that point, I didn't care what happened. I didn't know if I was going to stand or walk ever again, and I hadn't seen my kids in what seemed like ages. I didn't want anybody to see me like this. If they took the tube out and I died, well, I was okay with it.

The doctor came in, looked at how much liquid was collected in the bag, and took my vital signs.

"I think you've probably had enough of this—do you want to get rid of the tube?"

"YES!" I could not write it big enough.

I nodded, and they got to work, prepping me for removal.

"This is probably going to sting a little," I was told, and he gently started to pull on the tube. My nose and throat felt like they were on fire as he pulled it out of my nose. I could feel it retreat from my stomach, up my esophagus, and out through my nostril. I had no idea the tube was that long. It was like watching a magician pulling scarves out of a hat. The tube kept going and going.

As the last bit of tubing was removed, I gasped as air rushed into my lungs. My nose burned, and my stomach hurt. Breathing is something I have always taken for granted until I found it hard to do. I could see my heart rate and blood pressure going back down to normal on the monitor as I felt an incredible amount of relief that things were going to get better. After the doctor left and the nurses cleaned me up, I weakly thanked them and drifted off to sleep.

I slept through the night for the first time in over two weeks. I knew I was asleep because I dreamed about lots of things—images seemed to come and go randomly. I dreamed about my kids, missing my family, and times where we were all together. At one point, I felt like I was floating above the bed, looking down at myself and wondering why I looked so broken and weak. Other dream parts were jumbled bits of television and movies I'd had playing in the hospital.

The next morning, I blinked as the sun started to shine through the window. I could hear activity out in the hallway as the morning shift arrived for duty, checked on their patients, and made sure everything was okay. Eventually, my door opened, and Peace walked in.

"Good morning, Mr. David. How did you sleep?"

7

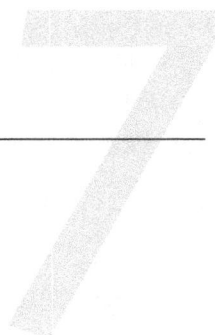

THE NEW ABNORMAL

Even if I was inside, the
world outside kept turning.

Over a few days, I began to adjust to the routine at the rehab hospital. I watched television, and visitors brought me books and magazines. I became a fan of watching old classic films and a whiz at math puzzles. Real food was slowly introduced back into the plan. I'd been on a clear diet for a while and was tired of eating gelatin and broth. I like chicken soup as much as the next guy, but it's even better when it includes chicken. As my tests improved, the doctor gave the approval to remove the catheter. Twelve hours later, everything was working normally, even if it was into a bedpan.

While my spinal fusion was healing, I couldn't do much by myself. Because of the fusion, my lack of strength, and the TLSO brace,

I needed help to do everything. I was still reduced to wearing a diaper. If the nurses were around, they'd help me in and out of my wheelchair for the bathroom.

One day, I felt the urge to go to the bathroom, so I rang the call button. Nothing. A few minutes later, I rang it again—still nothing. Things got urgent. After about twenty minutes, I realized I was either going to have to go where I didn't want to or get myself into the chair. Using every piece of available arm strength, I pushed my upper body into a vertical position, then used everything else to swing my legs out and transfer myself over into the chair.

I sweated as if I'd run a marathon. I inched my way into the wheelchair, hoping I didn't slip, fall, or crash to the floor. I also hoped the chair didn't roll away from me just as I was trying to get into it. Closer— closer—and with one final push, I landed with a big thump into the chair. I sat for a minute as I caught my breath and remembered why I got into the chair in the first place.

I unlocked the wheels and rolled forward toward the foot of the bed. Once I cleared the end, I carefully pivoted around the bed and turned toward the bathroom. Twelve feet away seemed like it was in the next county. I inched toward the bathroom, praying I would get there in time. There was still no sign of a nurse or orderly, so I was on my own, and now, I was determined to get there, even if I failed in the attempt.

I made it across the room and wheeled myself over the threshold of the bathroom. I positioned the chair and locked the wheels. I struggled to hoist myself over the toilet with every last available bit of strength. Just when I thought I wasn't going to make it—success.

I've rarely been so happy in all my life. Joyful tears streamed down my face. If I could go to the bathroom on my own, I might be able to get some dignity back. When I finished, I was able to clean myself up, wash my hands, and fix my clothes. I hoisted myself back into the chair, eventually made it back across the room, and reversed the procedure to get myself back into the hospital bed. Even though it was a considerable effort to get out of bed, across the room, and in the bathroom, the return trip seemed easier.

Later, Peace came into the room to check on me. "Do you need any help going to the bathroom?"

"Not anymore."

A worried look came to her face. Then she saw me with the first smile she had witnessed since I came into the hospital.

"You didn't go to the bathroom all by yourself, did you?"

"Yes, I did!" I said, feeling as proud as toddlers do when they finally figure out they can go to the bathroom on their own.

"Give me a high five!" Smiling, Peace held out her hand.

I started to slap her hand when she quickly pulled back and said, "You did wash your hands, didn't you?"

"Yes, I washed my hands!" We both laughed in triumph.

Over the next few days, I got into the routine of the rehab hospital. I wasn't quite ready for the hard stuff, but I was given little exercises to do, like squeezing a rubber ball or flexing my feet in the chair to start working on training my muscles to work again. Going to the bathroom became a routine event, for which I was thrilled. I depended on others for a lot of things, but having this one thing to myself made me feel slightly more human.

The food at the hospital was never Michelin Guide-worthy, but I got used to it and was even given the freedom to choose some of the menu items. I burned through math puzzles like they were going out of style, and I was finally able to take visitors. Maggie came first.

"I brought your satellite radio, along with something more useful."

I looked into the bag she was carrying and saw a stack of books, including the *Lord of the Rings* trilogy. "Aw, do I have to read?"

Maggie smiled and said, "It's good for you. Builds character." I had time to read since I was going to be there for a while. The radio made the days pass more quickly since I could listen to music, comedy, or the news.

My boss even came to visit—at first, we talked about the accident and recovery, but then I also saw he brought a bunch of employee appraisal paperwork. My accident occurred at the same time as the annual review deadline; I provided my input, and he was able to finish the work for me.

Eventually, my kids came to visit. The first time was a bit scary for all of us. My daughter initially hid behind her mother, and my son looked anxious. I hadn't seen them for over a month, and the hospital can be an intimidating place. Over a few visits, though, it became a welcomed relief for everyone and seeing the kids made me realize there was life outside of the hospital.

Even if I was inside, the world outside kept turning, and I needed to work hard to become a part of it again, whatever form that took.

8

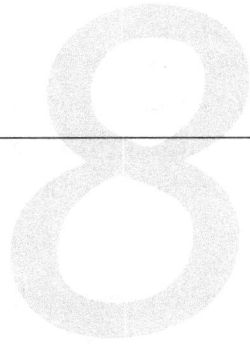

STANDING, STILL

Well, would you look at me.
I'm standing, still.

As I got stronger, the physical therapy assignments became tougher. I had not stood on my own in over a month. Each day, I'd roll out to the elevator and go downstairs for physical therapy. The initial exercises were easy—flexing my feet, raising my lower leg, or even wiggling my toes. Every exercise, no matter how small, was an important step. Because my long-term capability wasn't yet known, I was introduced to some tools to make life easier to manage. I was already grateful for the familiar handrails in the bathroom. The occupational therapist introduced me to other devices, like sock aids that allowed me to put on and remove socks without bending over. She also taught me how to use a grabber tool that helped me retrieve dropped items or things too far away to pick up.

Physical therapy was conducted in a large room that, at first glance, looked like it might be used for gymnastics. There were parallel bars, rings, and mats everywhere. After watching, it was clear none of the participants were ready for the Olympics. There were patients with all kinds of challenges, from knee replacements and minor injuries to others like me, or even those recovering from a stroke or traumatic brain injury.

Everybody had their own set of challenges, and I was no exception. I hadn't put any weight on my legs for over a month, and they were visibly thinner than before the accident. My physical therapist, BJ, was friendly but stern. She let me know from the first time we met that she was going to be pushing me to my limits. BJ taught me how to get in and out of my wheelchair more easily and turn myself over in bed. I learned how to do things that gave me more independence while in my wheelchair.

After a couple of weeks, BJ said, "It's time to get you out of that chair."

"What do you mean?"

"You're going to stand up."

I thought, *No way!*

I'd been in a wheelchair for a month and had no strength in my legs. BJ wasn't going to let me off easily. She put a harness on my upper body and locked my wheelchair in place.

"Let's work on getting up."

She stood on one side to steady me, and the harness kept me from falling. I braced my arms on the wheelchair and moved the footrest out of the way. I took a deep breath and started to push up—and—nothing. I fell back in the chair.

"Get up," said BJ.

"I can't."

"Get up."

I put my arms down, pushed, pushed, and pushed—and fell back in the chair.

"I can't do this, BJ."

"You're not getting out of here until you stand up."

"I can't."

"Do it again."

Over and over, I tried to push up, and each time, I'd fall back into the chair. I kept begging to quit, and BJ kept pushing me further. After about twenty tries, I said I'd try once more, but that was it. I gripped the arms of the wheelchair and pushed my weight forward. BJ steadied me from the side. My face turned red as I strained to make my legs work like they hadn't in over a month. I bit my lower lip as I held my breath, pushing harder, and harder, when suddenly—I locked my knees into place and stood. BJ held my shoulders tightly.

"You did it!"

"Yeah, because you weren't going to let me go back to my room until I did."

She smiled and helped me sit back down and catch my breath.

"Now, do it again."

Not wanting to prolong this torment, I shakily stood again, locking my knees in place and holding onto the rails for dear life. I could feel the harness tighten up as I tottered back and forth on my quaky legs. I stood four times before I finally collapsed into the chair.

"Not a bad job today, David. I'll see you in the morning."

She disconnected the harness, and I wheeled myself to the elevator and back to my room.

Trying to stand was scary. I was afraid I couldn't do it again, but now I'd succeeded four times in one day. I thought about all of the times I'd taken that ability for granted. I'd never thought about it much until it was taken away. Over the next week, I stood again and again. I didn't go anywhere other than up and down. It became a game to see if I could get myself vertical before BJ had to growl to get me moving.

I started to use the parallel bars to get in and out of the chair. I continued to work on my other exercises, building my arm and leg strength, wondering when I might be able to do more than stand. In some ways, it was enough for now. It made getting in and out of bed easier, and it certainly simplified bathroom visits. I couldn't take a shower yet, but I was able to do a better job of washing myself and managing self-care. I even started interacting with other patients, and my mood improved enough to take more visitors.

My sister flew in from the Midwest for a few days. Her visit made me feel even more like I wanted to get back to real life.

After two months, I'd had several visitors from work, my neighborhood, and even my hometown. I didn't like being in the hospital, but at least I was making progress. It seemed like ages since the night of the accident, even though it had only been eight weeks. I started to wonder how long I'd be in the hospital, and for the first time, I considered what it might be like to go home soon.

Physical therapy continued to build my strength, and BJ kept pushing me harder. Eventually, I pushed up out of the chair, and thought, *Well, would you look at me. I'm standing, still.*

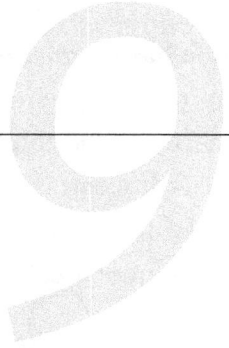

9

LIFE HAPPENS

Take it from someone who's been there.
Sometimes, it can happen to you.

When I got on my motorcycle on July 9, 2004, I had no idea what was about to happen. Had it gone slightly differently, I could have walked away from the accident, been permanently paralyzed, or worse. As it was, I'd suffered a devastating injury, and it took months of rehabilitation in the hospital to stand and walk a few feet.

Since then, I've learned:

To move forward, you have to **Identify the Obstacle**. Some obstacles are physical, like my accident and injury. Other obstacles may be emotional, like low self-esteem, a troubled childhood, or a challenging relationship. Obstacles might be financial, circumstantial, or any number of factors. To move forward, we have to identify the obstacle that's in our way. Until we do, we will stay stuck where we are.

Life has no guarantees. Each day is a gift, and what we do with it is up to us. We go about our daily business and routine because life is mostly predictable, and we never accept that the bad thing will happen to us. It seems it is someone else who has that unfortunate mishap, bad luck, or sobering diagnosis. Take it from someone who's been there. Sometimes it can happen to you.

Your life can change in an instant. I went from being a careful and confident new rider to an invalid in less than a couple of seconds. I never considered what might happen if I lost the ability to walk because that possibility never occurred to me. Once I went over the handlebars, it didn't matter whether I thought about it or not. My life changed. That doesn't mean you should anticipate disaster daily. Instead, I'm grateful for what I have today.

We need other people. I've spent a lot of my life being stubborn and independent. The truth is, I could not have recovered or survived without significant help from other people. I'm grateful for Sam, who called 911 and stayed with me until the paramedics arrived. From my surgeon, Dr. Childs; to BJ, my physical therapist; to Peace, my rehab nurse—I benefitted from their help. No matter how independent we think we are, we are all connected.

Once you identify the obstacle, the path becomes much clearer. Every day we're on this planet, things happen that are beyond our control. Some are good, and some much less so. The question isn't, "What's going to happen?" but, "How do we deal with what happens and make the best of it?"

After close to three months in the hospital, I realized how much I missed my family, my job, and my own bed. I knew life was going to be different when I left and wondered what life would be like if I could never walk again without some sort of assistance.

My next physical therapy goal was to get out the door.

PART TWO

START WITH A SINGLE STEP

10

FIRST STEPS

*It was all I could do to bring my
left foot forward and stop.*

Every day, BJ, my physical therapist, pushed me a bit further. She'd assess how I was doing and adjust her approach depending on what it took to get me moving in the right direction. Some days she'd start off easy, but others, she'd launch into me like a female R. Lee Ermey, the drill instructor from the movie *Full Metal Jacket*. I didn't know which version I was going to see when I wheeled myself down to the PT floor, but knowing I could get "Gunnery Sergeant BJ Hartman, my senior PT instructor" was usually enough to get me in motion.

After a few days of just getting up and down, BJ said, "Okay, enough standing in place; we're going to get you moving forward."

She directed me over to the parallel bars and had me lock down my wheelchair brakes. I pushed out of the chair and slid my left foot forward. Keeping a lot of weight on my arms, I then pulled my right leg forward and slowly shuffle-scooted my way to the end of the parallel bars. When I got to the end, BJ had me turn around and do the same thing back to my wheelchair. By the time I got in sixteen feet of shuffle-stepping and arm-walking, all I could do was collapse back in the wheelchair, covered with sweat.

I felt that was enough for the first day of actual forward motion. After a couple of days, I graduated to something I thought I wouldn't use for another forty years: a walker, complete with the neon green tennis balls on the front legs.

"You're kidding, right?"

"Time to move up to something more your speed."

I gave her a side-eyed glare but knew she was giving me a good-natured push in the right direction. Instead of hand-walking the parallel bars, I lifted my feet slightly off the floor and took actual steps, even if most of my weight was supported by the walker. Each time, I'd push a little bit farther, until I could make it the full twenty feet across the room.

"Time to take off your training wheels," said BJ.

"What?"

"Let's ditch the walker."

"You've *got* to be joking!"

"You know me. I don't do jokes—I'll be here to catch you if you need it."

Slowly, and with a lot of trepidation, I stood in place as BJ pulled the walker about three feet in front of me. I felt glued to the floor, afraid to even budge, for fear I'd fall to the floor like an overturned plate of spaghetti. It was all I could do to bring my left foot forward and stop.

"Well, that was half a step. Now bring your right foot forward."

I took a deep breath and fixed my eyes on the walker as a target, just in case. I pointed myself toward the door and cautiously moved my right leg forward and stopped. It was my first unassisted step in over two months.

BJ started clapping. "You did it!" she shouted.

"Now, take another one."

I took one step, two steps, then ten steps with the walker just out of reach until it was all I could do. For now, it was enough.

Every day, I'd wheel myself back up to my hospital room, and Peace would be there to ask how I did that day. Some days were better than others, but she always had a smile and a positive attitude, no matter what kind of day I had. She made sure I knew about any visitors, phone calls, or cards and letters I got.

I also got to know a little bit about her family and her life in Ghana before she came to the US. Even though I had a lot of challenges in front of me, some of those seemed to pale in comparison to the struggles she went through to make a new life in this country. But Peace never complained, no matter how grouchy I got. She'd just gently remind me that I looked like I was doing better, even if she didn't know what kind of progress I was making downstairs.

I continued to make progress, even though I could only walk about ten feet unassisted. Over time, I could walk multiple stretches of ten feet or a lap around the interior of the room. BJ started working with me on more practical tasks. She reminded me that I would go home at some point and would need to do a lot more than what we were working on in physical therapy.

At first, the idea of going home was difficult to comprehend after being gone for ten weeks. The hospital began to feel like home. But I missed my family terribly, and that gave me a bit of a boost to keep working harder in physical therapy.

In the PT room, they had a cutaway passenger car interior, where I practiced opening the door, transferring out of my wheelchair and climbing in and out of the car, closing the door, and putting on my seatbelt. Then I practiced it in reverse. I worked on that consistently because I really missed driving a car and wanted to get back to it.

We worked on skills I'd need in the real world, like stepping up and down off a curb, pushing a shopping cart, and reaching for items on shelves. We practiced how to get myself up from the floor in case I fell. I had to use a lot of arm strength and sweat to do it, but eventually, I could get myself up off the floor, if I really had to.

Over time, I got to know some of the other patients in physical therapy. I met an older gentleman who suffered a stroke and lost the use of his left arm and leg. I met a younger man who'd been in a motorcycle accident and hadn't worn a helmet. Seeing what challenges he faced made me grateful that I was wearing mine. I met a landscape laborer who'd fallen off a ladder. We were all at different ages with unique physical obstacles, but we shared in the battle to get well and improve our strength enough to take at least the first steps toward getting back to normal.

Back to normal.

I thought about that a lot, wondering what the new normal might be. My life, as well as my family's, was turned upside down by this. At some point, I'd be going home, and I'd have to learn how to adjust to the rest of the world, taking things one step at a time. It was hard to think about how far I still had to go, so I focused on the first steps in front of me.

But for now, it was enough.

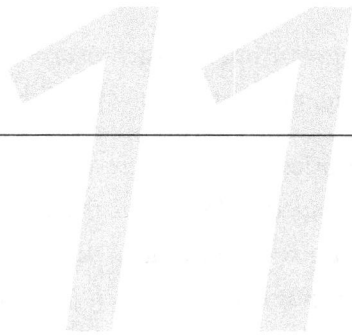

HULKING OUT

Anger can be a scary emotion.
It can also be useful.

Since the day of my accident, and throughout my time in the hospital, I experienced a range of emotions. Some days, when I wasn't making progress, I felt depressed. Other days, I felt excited when I reached a new level in PT. Some days, I was bored, and other days flew by. The one emotion I didn't expect to encounter as much as I did was anger. Anger is an interesting emotion. Some things are worth getting angry about, while others seem like a waste of time because no matter how angry you get, it doesn't improve the situation.

As soon as I was stable enough in rehabilitation to have time to think, I got angry a lot. I was angry about a number of things—angry at the motorcycle, angry at the curb, but mostly, angry at myself for getting into this mess. Angry at myself for putting my family through this.

Angry at pretty much everything. I even got angry at BJ from time to time, pushing back when I thought she was driving me too hard.

I noticed others were angry with me, too. Maggie was angry about having to take on all the burden of the kids and running the house along with coming to visit me. She was angry about my taking a risk that put my own life in jeopardy and the family's stability in danger. I don't blame her. It may have been an accident, but some choices come with risks and potentially devastating impacts that can be life-changing or life-ending.

When I was a young child, anger was something to fear. I grew up in a family where anger was a bad thing. Nobody ever blew up, lost their cool, or yelled at someone else. If they did, it was highly frowned upon and seen as a lack of control. Sometimes, however, anger jumped out when I least expected it, in a fight between siblings, or worse, a parent losing their composure and using a paddle to spank an errant child.

While I may have grown up in a generation where spanking was common, it was still a shocking and frightening moment when it happened. I learned that making mistakes sometimes led to punishment. I learned that getting upset or angry also led to punishment. Anything that stepped out of the expected behavior or didn't meet the standards could lead to being physically disciplined.

Anger can be a scary emotion.

It can also be useful.

In the first Marvel *Avengers* movie, Dr. Bruce Banner's character turns into The Hulk when he gets angry and loses control. By the end of the film, the team of Avengers needs him to turn into The Hulk to help them battle an overwhelming enemy.

CHAPTER 11

Captain America says, "Now might be a really good time for you to get angry."

As Dr. Banner walks toward the oncoming battle, he looks over his shoulder and says, "That's my secret, Cap. I'm always angry."

Hulking out, he jumps into the battle.

I thought about that for a long time. Anger can be scary, but if it's focused and directed on the right target, it can be incredibly useful. I started to get angry daily. Not at me, or BJ, or Maggie. Not at the motorcycle or my bad fortune, but angry at the obstacle right in front of me. Sometimes it was the next step forward. Sometimes it was going from four stairs to five. Whatever obstacle was in the way of my progress became the focus of my anger, and I would "Hulk out" daily. I never turned green or ripped my shirts, but I would bear down, grit my teeth, and even growl at myself to push myself just one more step.

I remember one day when I was working on climbing stairs. I could only go up three or four steps at a time. Maggie was helping watch me during my PT work, and she was angry. I would try to stop after a couple of attempts, and that was not going to work for her. She kept pushing me verbally, egging me on, and eventually said, "You got into this mess, and you're going to have to get yourself out," before storming out the door, leaving early.

I stood there, speechless, holding on to the handrail, watching as she walked toward her car. I had never seen her this angry in my life.

And it seemed to work. Getting angry made me progress much faster than I would have if I'd have stayed passive and waited for someone to help. Some days I needed to ask for help, but if I hit the floor, I was not going to ask unless there was no other way to get up. I got angry. I pushed harder. I got up—and tried again.

A funny thing happened. All this anger I was using up on my obstacles seemed to take it away from the other potential recipients. Both Peace and BJ noticed my mood was much better outside of PT, or when I finished another hard session. Maggie and the kids noticed my mood improve and started to visit more often. My new perspective about anger, where it could be a force for good, was a fantastic revelation for me. Anger wasn't something to be feared; it was something on which to be focused. It was a tool I could use to channel my frustrations into forward progress.

Ever since then, I haven't feared anger, whether it's mine or someone else's. If someone seems angry with me, I will attempt to see if I've done something that merits the anger, but if it's just someone having a bad day, I assume they're angry near me rather than at me. It's not something to take personally. The same goes for me getting angry around other people. I try to make sure I'm doing something positive to resolve the situation rather than stewing in my own frustration or venting at someone who doesn't deserve it.

It doesn't mean I don't get angry—I do—sometimes more often than I'd like. But my secret weapon is choosing the right target for the anger.

I try to use it for good.

12

PEACE OUT

Slowly, bit by bit, I took
a step. Then another.

Peace had been there since my first day at the rehab hospital. It was getting close to three months since the accident, and I talked with her more than anyone else, including my family and visitors. Since she saw me every day, she got to see my mood changes, but she didn't see all the improvement that was happening down in physical therapy. She was smiling a lot more, which meant I was doing better.

Most of my PT work was on the first floor of the hospital. Every morning after breakfast, I'd wheel over to the elevators and push the button, and when I rolled into the elevator, I'd give Peace a wave as I headed down. I'd come back a couple of hours later, sometimes frustrated, usually tired, and in no mood to deal with other people.

Peace was always smiling when I returned, asking me how it went. No matter how grouchy I was, she was a ray of sunshine in what was frequently a difficult place. One day, as I was wheeling about the rehab floor, I said to Peace, "Watch this."

Peace put down her clipboard and watched as I locked my wheelchair brakes and put up the footrests. I took a deep breath, gripped the arms of the wheelchair, and gave a push. Rocking back and forth, trying to make sure I didn't sway too far, I stood in place for what seemed like an eternity, but it was only a few seconds.

Slowly, bit by bit, I took one step, then another. Right . . . left . . . right . . . left as I inched my way around the nurses' station in the middle of the floor. I got to the end of the station and carefully angled to the left to make the turn. I wobbled a little bit but was able to keep going.

I made it to the next counter end and angled left again—halfway around—and started looking for the next turn. I began to tire a bit and felt a little shaky, but I kept going. When I turned the fourth corner, I started targeting my wheelchair, wondering if I could make it back to the seat before my legs gave out.

My right leg was starting to tremble a bit, as my muscles began telling me I'd gone a bit farther than my legs wanted to take me. With only a few more feet to go, I kept saying to myself, "Right . . . left . . . right . . . left . . ." as I got closer. At this point, if my legs gave out, I might be able to make a grab for the chair and still make it.

As I took one final step, I put my hands out, grabbed the armrests, turned, and collapsed back into my wheelchair. I sat for a minute, sweating and breathing heavily, and finally looked back up at Peace.

"What do you think?"

Peace didn't say anything, but I could see her eyes glistening, and a single tear running down her cheek. That told me more than she could have ever put into words.

She saw me come in, completely disabled, vomiting blood, and getting intubated, and helped me at my lowest possible point. She had to deal with assisting with the bathroom, chair, and turning me over in my hospital bed.

During that entire time, she never complained once. She did her job every day and made sure I was doing well. She listened to me gripe and complain but never criticized me about feeling down. Instead, she would distract me or change the subject until I got rid of whatever frustration I was experiencing.

Over the next few days, I started talking with the rehabilitation team about going home. My kids were already in school, and I'd missed my daughter's first day of kindergarten. While it was early September, the leaves were already beginning to turn, which signaled it was time for me to move on to the next stage.

I wrapped up my PT exercises with BJ, who now smiled more than growled at me. She was proud of the progress I'd made but cautioned that I'd need to work a lot harder once I got home. She wouldn't be there to push me, and I'd have to find the drive to keep myself working. Still, I was grateful for all the times she made me work when I didn't want to. She knew exactly when to push and when to back off.

I spent time with each member of the team, the orthopedic specialists, occupational therapist, psychologist, and even the orderly staff. I'd been there so long; we were all on a first-name basis. I had the opportunity to thank them and to imagine how much work everybody had put in on my behalf. If they hadn't worked so hard, I wouldn't have come so far.

On the last day, I got all my belongings packed, and Maggie arranged to pick me up. It was a long drive across the county to the hospital, but since I knew she was on her way, I found Peace working over forms at the nurses' station.

"Peace, I'm never good at goodbyes, and I wish there was something more that I could say besides 'thank you,' but I really do want to thank you for everything you've done during my time here," I said. "And please don't take this the wrong way, but if things go well, I don't want to have to see you again—at least not here."

Peace smiled and gave me a knowing hug. As she left work that day, she stopped by.

"When you got here, I didn't know if you were going to make it through the night, but I think now you are going to go where you want to go."

Maggie called from the car to let me know she was downstairs in the hospital lobby. Peace helped me gather my things, then rode the elevator down to the first floor with us as I carried my bag of hospital items on my lap. I was able to change into a T-shirt and shorts instead of my normal hospital-issued wardrobe. It felt good to wear my own shoes instead of hospital socks. I wheeled out the doors of the hospital, squinting at the sun, breathed in the fresh air, and rolled up to Maggie's car. I opened the door and expertly slid into the passenger seat.

I looked back at Peace, gave her a wave as I closed the door, clicked my seatbelt into place, and closed my eyes as Maggie drove us toward home. It was the end of a significant stage of my life. I tried to imagine what the next part might be like. I wouldn't have BJ or Peace around to push me, and I had to get to know Maggie and the kids all over again. I drifted off to sleep in the car, wondering what might come next.

Peace out.

13

BACK HOME AGAIN

Home is where things are safe.
Home is where we're protected.

After two months in the rehab hospital, I was discharged and sent home. I wasn't back to my pre-accident condition, but I could stand, sit, and walk a few steps around the house. I got used to the routine of being upright but also had many limitations. I could walk across a room but was happy to sit down once I reached the other side. I used my walker as well as portable handrails in the bathroom. It wasn't an ideal situation, but it was good to be home.

The thing I was most grateful for was to be around my family every day. Even though I wasn't home at the start of the school year, now I could help send the kids off to school and welcome them when they got home—being around them daily improved my mood considerably.

The cats even remembered who I was—especially when I took over feeding them. Being around the family and neighbors helped me feel somewhat normal. The neighbors brought meals we could quickly heat up, thus lightening the workload Maggie had shouldered for three months.

My sister came to visit, which was helpful. She was a stickler for order and cleanliness and was good about taking on a surrogate-parent role when the kids (or I) got too tired or grumpy.

I wasn't allowed to go back to work, but my boss would occasionally call with questions, which I was happy to answer. Being home alone all day was pretty boring, and I welcomed the opportunity to do something engaging, even if I didn't actually do "work."

While I could not walk far or drive, I was able to go places in a car if someone else was behind the wheel. I could get a cheeseburger at McDonald's—one of the little things that made me feel more human. I tried to focus on doing as many normal things as possible, like going to the bathroom, shaving, or getting in and out of a chair.

I've discovered through talking with other people who have gone through similar experiences that the big challenges were not so much the physical ones but adjusting *mentally* to how we felt *internally* and how we dealt with other people. The longer I stayed in the hospital, the more dependent and less capable I felt. Even though I gained skills and strength in physical therapy, I was still dependent on others to prepare meals, perform tasks, and give personal care.

It felt strange to be home at first and even smelled different than what I was used to in the hospital. There was no 24/7 nursing team on duty, and no one to come running in the night if I needed help. I had to realize that Maggie did the work of two parents and the best way for me to help was to take on whatever roles I could and work on getting better as quickly as possible. The kids needed both of us.

CHAPTER 13

Home. Just the sound of the word made me feel a sigh of relief. Every time I've gone on vacation or an extended business trip, returning home was the part of the journey where I finally got to relax and let down my defenses. It was the same in this case, but I had to relearn what the word meant for me now.

Maggie and kids had built their own routines since they'd been on their own for nearly three months. Now, I became an extra ingredient in the mix and needed to figure out where I fit in. In addition to dealing with the jobs of school, pets, and running the household, everybody else had to deal with my recovery and limited ability to keep up.

I felt like an outsider in some ways. It was my house—I lived there and was part of the family, but I frequently felt like an intruder. My life had changed pretty dramatically in comparison to the rest of the family. I tried my best to fit in and contribute where I could, but it was still a challenge.

I tried to make up the duties where I could. If I couldn't take out the trash or bend over to empty the dishwasher, I could read to the kids at bedtime. I could ask them about their school day and assist with homework. It may have been only three months, but the kids had both grown taller and seemed older than the time that elapsed. It took us some time to get reacquainted and for all of us to get used to me being home again.

I thought about families who had to deal with that challenge all the time—soldiers get deployed for long periods away from their families, and their children learn to deal with their parent's absence.

One night, when I put Lauren to bed, she looked nervous when I started to leave.

"Lauren, are you okay?"

"Daddy, are you going to go away again?"

"What makes you think that?"

"I'm just scared."

Even if I thought the kids were fine, I didn't realize I had to deal with their fears that I might not return home. I was taken from them suddenly, and I'm sure it was on their minds as a recurrent possibility. I tried to reassure them I wasn't planning on going away anytime soon and would certainly not be getting on a motorcycle again, but I could hear the uncertainty in their voice whenever they asked me about going away.

"Lauren, I can promise you: I'm not getting on a motorcycle ever again."

I hugged her and turned out the light. I stood in the hallway for a while, trying to think about how my accident and absence affected the rest of the family.

Still, I was home. While I might go away from time to time, I gained a new appreciation of what it meant to come home. Home is where things are safe. Home is where we're protected. I knew I needed to make sure my kids knew I wasn't going to leave them, and as I recovered, I'd try to make it up to them as best I could.

14

MAILBOX TO A MILE

Each day, I'd do the mailbox relay.
I got to know the neighbors well.

When I got home from the hospital, I'd only been walking for a short distance—ten to twenty feet at a time. Dr. Childs told me walking was one of the best ways to build up my strength, so that's what I did. On the first day home, I decided to walk all the way to the next-door neighbor's mailbox.

I never thought eighty feet seemed far, but that day, it felt like a transcontinental journey. Even stepping out the front door was an adventure, because I had to take two steps down to the sidewalk without any handrails to hold.

Even though I ran a lot previously, a few steps winded me now. I took breaks every few feet as I got lightheaded and needed time to catch my breath. At this point, I was less concerned with being an Olympic athlete than I was reaching my own mailbox without keeling over.

Once I reached my mailbox, I held on and rested, and eyed the neighbor's mailbox eighty feet away. Now, that might not seem far, but for me, it seemed like it was more than I could achieve. I told myself that if I had to, I could call someone with my cellphone if I got tired, or if I felt like I could not make it back to the house. I hated to think what would have happened if I fell down.

I set my gaze on the neighbor's mailbox in the distance. Pushing off of my mailbox, I started slowly moving forward, step by step. I kept my eyes locked on it, and once I passed the halfway point, I knew I had to get to the mailbox to have something to push off of and get me back home. It's the same feeling I had when swimming laps in the pool. Having that wall to push off from made me feel a lot better about making it to the other side.

I was unsteady, gently rocking back and forth, but I kept taking steps. With only a few more to go, I knew I'd make it there but wasn't sure if I'd be making a final reach at the finish line. With one more lurch, I reached out and held onto the neighbor's mailbox as if it was my long-lost friend. Sweaty and shaking, I was happy to make it unscathed.

Now, I had to turn around and do the same distance back home. Another eighty feet. Each day, I'd do the mailbox relay. I got to know the neighbors well. If I wasn't out there, they'd remind me that I needed to get my steps in. I started with one mailbox, then two. Each time, I'd try to go a little bit farther.

Some days, I'd push a little too hard and wonder if I was going to get back home. I was usually shaky by the time I did. The reward was to sit in my leather recliner and watch television. I never was a big television watcher, but collapsing in a chair after that effort and turning on some mindless entertainment was a nice reward.

CHAPTER 14

Each day, I'd try to get to one more mailbox. One day, I got to my turnaround point and thought, *I'm going to go all the way around the block.* I slowly walked to the corner, and instead of turning around, turned left; now there was no turning back.

There were a couple of times I had to stop, but each step got me closer to the house. I kept reminding myself that the distance was getting shorter and shorter. Besides, I didn't have my phone with me. I'd have to ring a doorbell and ask for help, which was the last thing I wanted to do.

I got to the next corner and turned left again. Now, it was just a short trek to my house. As I got closer, I gained a little bit of confidence. I also noticed the slightest change in grade or elevation. It might not seem like a hill, but even a single degree change was noticeable.

The last few yards toward the house were at a slight downhill grade. I picked up a minor bit of speed and turned into the driveway. Feeling a bit stiff, I lumbered up the sidewalk, reached the front steps, turned, sat down on the steps, and cried.

I knew I wasn't ever going back to where I started.

Every day after that, I used that feeling to push farther. The block was a half-mile, and eventually, I got up to three-quarters of a mile, then I walked a full mile. I graduated to two times around the block. The neighbors gave me encouragement by honking their horns as they drove by, which made me feel more confident. Some neighbors honked at me when I was crossing the street. I could not tell if they were offering support or wanting me to get out of the way. I told myself they were helpful.

I traveled farther from home and gained confidence over time. I couldn't do much more than a mile at one time, but I'd go out multiple times a day. I grew my totals to two miles, then three miles, and by December, I walked up to seven miles every day. Looking back, progress was slow, yet it was always forward.

With all the walking, I began to sleep better. I'd come in from the last walk of the day and hit the shower, and once I dried off and climbed into bed, I was out and sleeping faster than the time it took to get into bed.

I'd occasionally wake up sore from the previous day's effort, but all in all, I felt good when I got out of bed in the morning. I was careful not to add so much effort in any one day to trigger a setback, but the little increases in the distance added up over time.

The hardest part of all of this walking wasn't the walking itself. It was getting up, getting off the couch, and getting out the door. Once I was in motion, the rest of it felt much easier. The most challenging part was convincing myself I had to get up—*now*.

15

ADJUSTING TO THE NEW "NORMAL"

*While a lot of things still felt strange,
I just wanted to be normal again.*

By the end of December, I could drive short distances and was released back to work. Driving was something I'd sorely missed. It's strange to think I was so dependent on it. Being able to drive on my own was a massive step in my independence, even though I was grateful for my new handicapped placard.

I could walk and do strength-building exercises, but I still wore my TLSO brace twenty-four hours a day. I removed it to shower, and that was about it. As soon as I could, I needed to put it back on.

It was a huge moment for me when I went back to work. Because I was classified as disabled, until then, I wasn't even allowed to look at email. I thought it was strange because my hands and eyes worked just fine. I made the mistake of telling the disability coordinator that I read work email, which made him go nearly apoplectic.

My first day in the office was a little overwhelming. I could drive in, park in the garage, and take the elevator up to my floor. The receptionist saw me step off the elevator and started to run up and give me a hug, but the brace seemed a little intimidating. I let her know it was okay; I wasn't going to break.

My boss was glad to see me back, as was my team. They all graciously took up the slack while I was out. Now that I was back in the office, they'd be able to focus more on their jobs and less on doing mine. Everybody I met at the office was enthusiastic to see me back. I told the same stories repeatedly. It seemed like everyone wanted to hear the details, even if I didn't feel like reliving the accident again and again.

I had to explain about the brace and my limitations. I always took someone up on their offer to help by opening doors for me or picking up things I dropped. I was careful not to drop any pens or paper at work because there was no guarantee I'd be able to get back up off the floor without assistance.

My first days were rather short. Initially, I was able to come in for a couple of hours, then extend the time as I got stronger. For the most part, the days were routine, and I liked how helpful it was to work from home a couple of days a week.

At home, I'd walk several times a day. As I walked more and built up more strength, I could sit without the brace and only had to wear it when I was standing for more than a few minutes. Eventually, I could sleep without the brace.

CHAPTER 15

The first night without the brace was a little scary, but I seemed to adjust after a few nights. I enjoyed being able to sleep all night and go straight to the shower in the morning without the brace. My surgical scar had healed, and even though it was itchy, I appreciated just standing under the showerhead and letting the hot water wash over me.

I also took advantage of the hot tub at the local recreation center. If I was sore from walking or physical therapy, it helped me relax my aching muscles. I was used to all the strange looks I got as I walked to the pool in my TLSO brace. When I noticed someone staring a bit too long, I made a game of asking them if they'd like to try it on. I didn't get any takers, but I did see a few red faces as they turned away. I chalked it up as part of the experience.

In March, I had to fly for business. I wondered how I'd manage the logistics of moving through the airport. At the metal detector machine, the TSA agent ordered me to take off the brace. I hadn't tried to stand often without it, so I didn't know what would happen. I feared I'd flop like a rusty door hinge.

Fortunately, there were no mishaps while I wore the brace. I enjoyed participating in normal life again. I was also surprised that my titanium spinal hardware did not set off the metal detectors. When I went through an x-ray machine, the operator could see that I was literally bolted together.

My time in the brace decreased to eight hours a day, then six, then four, and by May, I only needed it if I was going to be on my feet a lot, or I felt tired while standing. I'd lost weight since the first fitting, so the brace was reformed and tightened, so it fit well enough to be useful.

I was also glad to say goodbye to my assist rails in the bathroom. I felt even more confident when I was able to get up and down reasonably well. I gained momentum as I tossed my crutches and cane in the garage where the walker sat gathering dust. I was happy to remove any reminder of my hospital stay as quickly as I could.

"Doctor, do I need to renew my handicap placard?" I asked Dr. Childs at my next visit.

"What do you think you need?"

"Really, I'd rather park like everybody else."

"You want to park that poorly?"

"Ha, ha, doc. Very funny."

"Let this one expire, and if you think you need it, come back in, and we can reevaluate."

"Fair enough, doc."

A problem I encountered when parking in a handicapped space was peer pressure. If I didn't have the brace on, I would get all sorts of dirty looks, a nasty note on my windshield, or even the occasional confrontation. More than once, I had to pull my shirt up to show my long scar to someone who didn't think I should be parking so close to the front of the lot.

While a lot of things still felt strange, I wanted to be normal again.

AS EASY AS RIDING A BIKE

It reminded me of when I was a kid,
and riding a bike felt like flying.

As I reached my one-year post-accident anniversary, I continued physical therapy less frequently.

"You've made great progress, David, so I think we're done," said Dr. Childs at my one-year follow-up appointment.

After major surgery, rehabilitation, and a year of healing and hard work, he released me from treatment. At first, I didn't know what to think. I was so glad to be walking, I hadn't considered any other forms of exercise. Post-accident, I never even thought of running, but I wanted to add a few exercise options, so I tentatively got back on the bicycle to try and ride around the neighborhood.

It was easier than I thought. While I was unsteady at first, the old lessons came back, and I rode farther each time. While I didn't need training wheels, I was glad to be able to put my feet down and stop whenever I could. I felt like I was riding for the first time, but before too long, my old bike skills came back.

I was happy enough to just cruise around the neighborhood. It gave me something different to do than walk all the time. Even within the neighborhood, I pushed a little bit farther each time. After a couple of months, I wanted to go beyond the local streets and ride some more challenging distances.

Northern Virginia has a large and active bicycle community with a nice network of trails close to where I lived. I figured out a quick way to get to the bike trails and enjoyed expanding my horizons to include the Washington and Old Dominion (W&OD) trail. It is a favorite of local riders and is filled with cyclists of all ages, runners, skaters, and walkers—with and without dogs, especially on weekends.

My first few rides were pretty short. I'd get to the trail, get a couple of miles in, then turn around. Over time, I started building my distance to an average ride of ten miles, but some days, I'd push it up to fifteen or even twenty. Each time I felt like I had a bit more freedom.

I started to get faster, too—not Tour de France fast, but fast enough. Occasionally, I'd be the one who passed; I'd call out, "On your left," and pass a slower rider. That was a huge boost to my confidence.

Slow and steady was the order of the day, though. I'd see large groups of organized riders fly by me like I was standing still. As they passed, I'd push to keep up. It usually didn't take long for them to drop me like a bad habit, even though it felt good to push myself.

CHAPTER 16

I rode a hybrid bike—meant for comfortable riding on smooth pavement. Once, a spandex-clad cyclist was riding on my tail, drafting off of me to make it easier to ride with less effort. I didn't mind it at first, but after a while, my inner Lance Armstrong became annoyed as he rode too close to my wheel for comfort. At the first opportunity, the wannabe racer pulled out to the left and pushed past me a little too close, brushing against my sleeve. He didn't bump into me, but it seemed he wanted to show off his cycling skills as he pulled away.

At this point, I wasn't just annoyed; I got angry. The trail picked up some rolling hills; I took advantage of the downward slopes, closing the distance. Even though I rode an upright bike, I was strong enough to push faster when I wanted to. After the third hill, I caught up and at the top of the hill, called out, "On your left!" and blew past him as I went on the downhill.

I was ahead of him for a couple of miles when he finally caught me near my turnaround point.

As he went by, he growled, "Anybody can go faster downhill."

"I caught you . . . going up."

I felt so good that the ride home just flew by. Over the next few months, I began to enjoy riding the bicycle. It reminded me of when I was a kid, and riding a bike felt like flying. Even on the days I was caught in the rain or had a flat tire, a bad day on the bicycle was better than a good day off of it.

I had some of those bad days, too. On one ride, I had no fewer than three flat tires. I replaced the first tube without incident, but evidently, I didn't check the tire for debris, so in less than a mile, I felt the tire go flat again. This time, I made sure the tire was clear, got it inflated, and was back on my way.

I must not have checked for a pinched tube, because about two miles away from home, I heard that awful *pssss* sound—flat again.

I'd used up all my spare tubes, and I did not have my phone.

I did the "walk of shame" those last two miles, walking my bike along the sidewalk until I rolled up to the house. I recycled my dead tubes and fixed the tire a fourth time. The next week, I put in tire liners to give me some additional protection from flats.

More than once, I got caught in the rain. A little bit of rain isn't bad; it can cool things down on a hot summer day. A lot of rain poses other challenges. It's hard to see through eyeglasses since they don't have windshield wipers. Brakes go from useful to non-existent, and you become even less visible to vehicles. More than once, when I got home, I dried off my bike with towels, then I'd enjoy a long hot shower to bring my body temperature back up to something resembling normal.

Each ride brought more confidence and a sense of adventure. There came a time where, after a long but satisfying ride, I thought, *Well, I may not be able to do everything—*

"But I can do this."

THE LONGEST JOURNEY

Point yourself in the right direction,
and you've already made progress.

Lao Tzu is credited with the phrase, "A journey of a thousand miles begins with a single step." I recalled this when I went into surgery, and Dr. Childs told me there was a possibility I may not walk again. Thanks to his competent work, Peace's encouragement, and BJ's constant pushing me just a little bit harder each day, I was able to take that single step. Each day, I made it a little bit further on that journey.

Even though it was a few months since the accident, and I was happy to be walking again, I started to think about where I wanted to go. In some respects, I felt like I had done enough. I was walking and felt like I had made it past the worst part. From a physical standpoint, I had. From a mental and emotional perspective, the journey was just beginning.

The lessons I learned in the hospital took a long time to sink in, but looking back, I learned several things:

The longest journey Starts with a Single Step. My body was on its way to healing, but some injuries are more than just physical. My journey was far from over. In fact, it was just beginning. No matter how short or long the path is, you've got to take the first step to get there.

You don't have to know the end of the journey to start. I had no idea where this new adventure was going to lead. When I was discharged from the hospital, I still used a walker at times. My goal each day was to be less dependent on it. But to go anywhere, I knew I had to get started.

You may not be strong, but you can get stronger. After surgery, I was barely able to wiggle my toes, but that was an improvement over the pre-surgery trauma. Every day, I came to appreciate that BJ pushed me just a little bit harder because I got stronger. Finally, I took my first step, and each day, I could do a little bit more. Before long, I walked across the room, down the street, and eventually, several miles a day.

Direction is more important than location. If you've ever been frustrated about your situation, you are not alone. I think everyone has times where they feel like they don't measure up to whatever external measure they're applying to themselves. The truth is, it doesn't matter where you start. Point yourself in the right direction, and you've already made progress.

Start with a single step, and you can get there. When I was building up my daily walking strength, my primary goal was to reach the neighbor's mailbox. After that, I added another mailbox each day, and before long, I was walking all the way around the block. It was hard work to build back my strength, but each day started by taking that first step.

PART THREE

COMMIT TO CHANGE

18

CLIMBING AND CRASHING

*The bike was damaged, and I
was scraped up quite a bit.*

In 2008, the motorcycle accident was four years behind me. I continued to increase my distance and enjoyed riding with other people. I upgraded from a hybrid bike to a genuine carbon fiber road bike and occasionally rode it twenty-one miles to the office a couple of days a week.

I did not know what I was capable of, and began to challenge myself. I rode with a local cycling group and improved from the slowest Ride Group (Group D) to the C Ride Group, and eventually to the B Ride Group. The A Ride Group consisted of people who actually raced, so I was happy and content to be a solid "B" student.

I rode my first twenty-five-mile ride and even worked on the Boy Scout cycling merit badge with my son, which culminated in a fifty-miler. I rode my first metric century (sixty-two-mile, one hundred-kilometer) ride. In 2007, I completed the Seagull Century, my first full century, one hundred-mile ride, in Salisbury, Maryland. The ride was completely flat, but hey—one hundred miles is one hundred miles.

I set my sights on the Assault on Mt. Mitchell (AOMM). It had always been a bucket list item, but now I considered it a possibility. The AOMM is a 102-mile ride that is relatively easy for the first seventy-three miles until it starts to climb toward the Blue Ridge Parkway and finishes at the top of Mount Mitchell, North Carolina. The total amount of climbing is over 11,000 feet, with most of that in the last thirty miles.

Over the fall, winter, and spring, I trained, climbed, and walked up a lot of hills to prepare for the event. I felt strong enough and ready for my first event in 2008. I did well for up to eighty-five miles before cramps and dehydration took their toll. At the entrance to the Blue Ridge Parkway, my cramped quads gave out, giving me no other option but to hitch a ride in a support vehicle to the top of the mountain. I was so embarrassed; I didn't tell people I quit—I let them think I had completed the whole ride. In retrospect, it would have been better to let my friends know the truth. I wasn't the first person to drop out of a challenging event and certainly wouldn't be the last.

I came home and got back into the routine—riding to work a couple of days a week. One day, riding the bike trail in Vienna, Virginia, I came up to a street crossing. It was a two-lane street that had big signs and flashing lights to alert the cars, but I took care not to depend solely on signs.

There was not much traffic, but I saw cars in the area, so I unclipped my foot from the pedals and coasted to a stop at the intersection. A car stopped on the right, waving me forward, but since I had been given wrong directions before, I held up a hand to thank the driver, then looked in the opposite direction for other cars.

The car coming the other way stopped, too, so it looked safe to go ahead. I clipped into the pedals and pushed forward, rolling into the crosswalk. There were now two cars stopped on the right, and two on the left, so I thought it would be safe to cross the street.

As I cleared the vehicle on my right and aimed for the trail just a few feet away, I heard the roar of an engine accelerating. I looked in the direction of the sound to my right, and I saw a Honda Civic rocketing toward me. Even though there were only two lanes, some guy came flying around all the cars, driving into the parking spaces to pass them on the right. I had no time to react and felt the bike being lifted into the air as the car plowed under me.

Still attached to the pedals, I landed on the hood. The bike and I went horizontal, and I hit the windshield with a big *thunk*. The car stopped, forcing me to slide down the hood to the pavement—still attached to the bike.

For a second, I tried to assess what had happened. I knew I'd been hit, but my first worry wasn't that—it was whether my legs still worked. I heard car doors opening and closing, the rush of footsteps. The driver who hit me tried to grab me and pull me up while I was still attached to the bike. I was so angry, and I literally growled at him to back off while I unclipped my feet from the pedals, pushed the bike away, and climbed up off the pavement.

The bike was damaged, and I was scraped up quite a bit. The police arrived, and then the paramedics. At least this time, I was standing. They took me and the bike away in an ambulance. I kept wiggling my fingers and toes all the way to the Emergency Room. Things looked like they still worked.

The bike was damaged, but repairable. And so was I.

At the hospital, I got the usual x-rays and MRIs. The verdict? I had a slight fracture to an upper vertebra from the impact, but not enough to cause any lasting damage. Mostly, I was scraped up with a few abrasions. In truth, the bike looked worse than I did.

I went back to driving to and from work. I was lucky. If the guy had been driving an SUV or big truck, I might not have made it. For his little Honda Civic, I served as a big, clumsy, temporary hood ornament.

The driver was cited for "Failure to Yield." I figured he would pay the ticket, but I got a notice in the mail that he was contesting the citation. I wondered how he thought that might work, or maybe he thought the police officer or I might not show at trial?

When I got to court, it was clear that the entire police force of Vienna, Virginia, was there to testify for their cases. I saw the driver for the first time since the accident but didn't introduce myself. I don't think he recognized me at all. When it came to his time to testify, he stated what I've heard a lot of drivers say: "I never saw him." He also testified that he thought I rode out into the intersection without looking, and he drove through the parking spaces to try and avoid hitting me. I kept silent until the judge asked me if I wanted to provide my version.

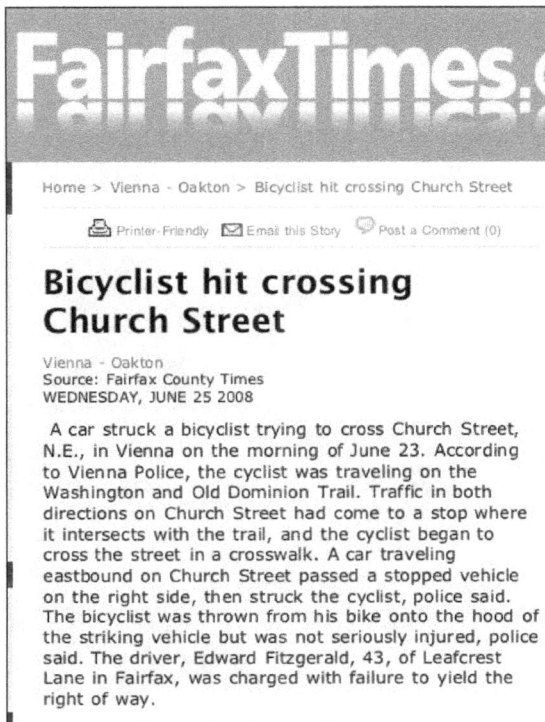

FairfaxTimes.

Home > Vienna - Oakton > Bicyclist hit crossing Church Street

Printer-Friendly   Email this Story   Post a Comment (0)

Bicyclist hit crossing Church Street

Vienna - Oakton
Source: Fairfax County Times
WEDNESDAY, JUNE 25 2008

A car struck a bicyclist trying to cross Church Street, N.E., in Vienna on the morning of June 23. According to Vienna Police, the cyclist was traveling on the Washington and Old Dominion Trail. Traffic in both directions on Church Street had come to a stop where it intersects with the trail, and the cyclist began to cross the street in a crosswalk. A car traveling eastbound on Church Street passed a stopped vehicle on the right side, then struck the cyclist, police said. The bicyclist was thrown from his bike onto the hood of the striking vehicle but was not seriously injured, police said. The driver, Edward Fitzgerald, 43, of Leafcrest Lane in Fairfax, was charged with failure to yield the right of way.

This isn't the way I wanted to make the news.

Instead of arguing against the driver's version of events, I pulled out a series of printouts. Whenever I rode my bike, I had a Garmin GPS with a heart rate sensor strap and cadence sensor that measured how fast I pedaled. As I turned the stack of paper over to the judge, I explained how the map showed my route of travel. The data showed me slowing down as I approached the intersection, coasting as I stopped pedaling and braked, and then stopping entirely for over one minute as my heart rate dropped.

I pointed to the big spike in the data where I went from traveling five miles an hour forward to twenty miles per hour sideways, and finally, where the data went blank.

"That, Your Honor, is where the driver struck me in the intersection," I stated matter-of-factly.

I looked over at the driver and saw him staring at the floor.

Even when intersections are well-marked,
it's important to be careful.

"Sir, would you like to rebut Mr. Hollingsworth's testimony?" the judge asked.

The man shook his head side to side, indicating he did not want to rebut it.

The judge banged his gavel.

"Guilty. Fine issued as per statute."

It took over three years to settle the civil case, but I got my bike replaced and my medical costs covered, and I also gained a better appreciation for watching out for other vehicles on the road.

Even if you look both ways and think the way is clear, it's a good idea to check one more time to make sure. Second chances are hard to come by, and I've had enough close calls that my cat wishes he had that many lives. I know in any confrontation with a car, I'm going to come out on the losing side of things, so I'm always expecting the unexpected.

19

FALLING APART

When I fixed one situation, another one
quickly flared up somewhere else.

Not all injuries are physical. After the motorcycle accident, it took a long time for me to feel safe or normal again. Even after that, some situations brought back memories of the crash and its aftermath in vivid detail.

I always felt safer when I was driving—not because I was a demonstrably better driver, but I felt if I was driving, at least I could have some control over my own destiny. I was never a good car passenger. When other people drove, I would wear out the armrest, dashboard, and carpeting from my gripping the door, pre-emptive bracing on the dashboard, and invisible braking to make sure we stopped. The 2008 bicycle accident only made my reactions worse.

A few years prior to the motorcycle accident, I crashed my car in a driving event at Summit Point Raceway. I wasn't racing. It was a driving improvement seminar, focused on building car control skills and driver confidence. None of that mattered when my brakes failed on a straightaway. The instructor and I rode the car into the woods, snapping off saplings and small branches as the vehicle came to a stop. There were no injuries, but the car was a total loss. The motorcycle accident brought back those memories whenever someone would stop too suddenly or drive too close to my car. I became much more nervous when driving to and from work.

Work became more difficult; the atmosphere became increasingly toxic when corporate politics began to become more important than actual work. Several of my colleagues left the company, leaving fewer friends for mutual support and making it harder to focus. In addition, with the accident a few years in the past, it somehow became acceptable to talk about it in negative terms. Several people started giving me the nickname "Crash." They may have meant it in a joking manner, but with the politically charged environment, it felt more like an insult. Those comments made it harder to feel positive about the job.

My company merged with a larger firm in 2009, which brought many changes to the environment, and most of them weren't positive. The merger was touted as an equal partnership, but it was clear from the start that the other company was taking the lead in the new structure. Over a period of a few months, my department was restructured with the new company in charge. My coworkers were replaced one by one.

I received an alarming call from another office peer who had just been laid off. He wanted to alert me that my job was next. Even with advance warning, it was still a shock to lose the job I had held for over ten years. It took several months to find something permanent, but I was able to get some consulting work that paid the bills. The new job didn't pay quite as much, but I liked that it was less stressful and closer to home.

CHAPTER 19

All the stress of the job transition distracted my focus away from exercising and eating right, and I started to gain weight, which added stress to my marriage. No marriage is perfect, and every couple has challenges, but ever since the accident, Maggie and I argued more often, and little disagreements became major disputes. She frequently brought up the accident as the reason she was so angry. For a lot of reasons, I didn't blame her.

Because I was so consumed by my recovery and returning to work, I sometimes lost sight of the impact the accident had on the rest of the family. I tried to do more things one-on-one with both children and do what I could to reassure them I was not going to do anything to put them in a situation where they would be without me again.

Despite taking time to focus more on home life, it did not seem to alleviate any of the marital tension. Gaining weight and not taking care of myself didn't help matters. Maggie told me I wasn't taking care of my health, and it was having a negative effect on her and the kids.

I agreed with her. I'd let my weight creep up as I dealt with the work stress by eating. I didn't drink or smoke, but my eating habits were unhealthy. I needed to seek outside support on improving them because I wasn't doing well on my own. During another discussion, while we were on a family vacation, I promised I would find a professional to work with me on the issue when we returned.

When we got back home, I looked up the names of potential therapists who dealt with stress eating or similar issues. I didn't get too far when the kids started acting out in school, and I was called in several times to deal with behavior issues. In the past, Maggie dealt with any school situations. I started taking the lead on those calls but quickly learned how much Maggie had been dealing with while I was in the hospital.

It took a lot of time, and I pushed dealing with my personal issues to the back burner.

When I was a child, I used to watch performers on television spinning plates while the "Sabre Dance" music played in the background. They would add more and more plates while the music got more intense, and eventually, some plates would crash to the ground. The performer would valiantly keep going, and while it was quite a spectacle, sometimes all the plates would crash in quick succession, bringing the action to a halt.

I seemed to be living a real-life version of plate-spinning. I'd chase one crisis after another, with plate after plate crashing to the ground. If I wasn't dealing with a work crisis, there was one at home. When I fixed one situation, another one quickly flared up somewhere else. If I focused on work, the family suffered, and if I took the time to deal with family issues, work suffered. In pretty much every case, I failed to focus on taking care of my personal health, which affected everything else.

After several months of various crises, I was constantly on edge and unable to focus on work or family. It showed in both places. One day, I came home from a difficult day at work, hoping to spend a more relaxing evening at home with my family. Happy to be home, I walked in the door.

Maggie met me in the kitchen and said, "I want a divorce."

20

ROCK BOTTOM

I looked in the mirror and
didn't like what I saw.

In late 2012, things were going from bad to worse. I'd survived the accident and recovery, but everything else seemed to go wrong. I lost a job I'd held for a decade and struggled in the new one. I wasn't in good physical health from all the stress, and my marriage was falling apart. Even though I could see things getting worse, I couldn't seem to assemble the emotional energy to turn things in a positive direction. Every day seemed to bring more stress and worry.

Maggie and I had struggled ever since I came home from the hospital. We argued about little things and disagreed on most of the big things. We fought about decisions on money, priorities, and even the kids. When she said she wanted a divorce, it became even more difficult to find common ground. Any discussion on a topic eventually turned toward divorce as the solution.

I'd initially sought out a therapist to help me get to the bottom of my stress eating, but now, the agenda changed dramatically. Instead of talking about why I continued to overeat, we discussed how to survive what was going on at home. My therapist reassured me that for now, surviving the present difficulty was enough.

Maggie was clearly angry about my decision to get a motorcycle and the risk I took by riding one. That's a natural fear to have, and I tried to respect those feelings by taking the responsible steps to become a safe rider.

However, eight years after the accident, there was nothing I could do to erase it. I could only apologize for what had happened in the past, and try to be better going forward. That didn't seem to be good enough. Maggie became angrier and started demanding I leave the house. I refused because I was involved in both kids' lives, with one child in scouting, and the other in art and creative endeavors. If I wasn't working, I was spending time with the kids.

I also refused to leave the house because, at the time, I didn't want a divorce. I knew things weren't good but was willing to try and work through the difficulty, or at least come to some sort of compromise to provide some semblance of stability for the kids. Getting a divorce would mean immediately spending a lot less time with them. From Maggie's reaction, I expected that time to be zero.

Every night, I'd help with dinner, spend time with the kids, and then go downstairs. By this time, we'd moved into separate bedrooms, and I tried to avoid Maggie because my presence seemed to agitate her to the point where it added to the children's stress.

My refusal to leave the house made the situation even more tense. While Maggie wanted me to leave, my attorney recommended I stay in the house and reduce any interaction with her. That sounded easy in the office but it was difficult to do at home. When conversations became heated, I tried to stay calm and not react, but the stress did get to me, too. To keep the situation from getting any worse, I started leaving the room whenever the discussion became less than civil.

So, I kept doing that at the expense of my own health. The stress of working toward a divorce, my job, and the day-to-day living in the situation led to more stress eating and weight gain. It was a poor coping mechanism, but I didn't feel like I had any better tools to deal with the stress. I felt like I was locked into a cycle of stress, stress eating, and weight gain.

I tried to defuse some of the stress with humor. That helped a bit at work but not at home. At home, I would put the kids to bed after dinner, then go downstairs to my office and work on the computer until I was too tired to stay awake. While on the computer, I would eat to deal with my feelings of stress and loss.

Some people go for alcohol, some for chocolate. I would bury my feelings inside a bag of potato chips. On the back of a bag, the calories are listed for each serving, which I always felt was a misnomer. Once I opened a bag of chips, the number of servings was always one. If I started eating a bag of potato chips, I was getting to the bottom of it. Being goal-oriented is generally positive, but not when it comes to emotional eating.

Looking back, I realize my eating was not just about dealing with the current emotional stressors. There was a lot of unresolved trauma from the motorcycle accident that I was hiding behind the activity of eating. If I was alone with my thoughts for too long, the memories of the accident would start to intrude in my thoughts. If I was eating, I didn't have to deal with the memories of the accident.

I knew I needed to change, but I'd convince myself that things weren't so bad. I'd lost weight before, and when I wanted to, I could take it off again. That worked for a while, but over time, I had to keep buying larger and larger clothes. I avoided looking at myself in the mirror and refused to be photographed because I didn't want to be reminded of my current reality.

I vividly remember the day I stepped on the scale, and it read 250.5 pounds. I am five feet, nine inches tall. This translated to a Body Mass Index (BMI) of thirty-seven—35 percent body fat. I had arrived. I was officially obese. I was disgusted and sad. At this point, I felt like I hit rock bottom, and nobody was going to change things for me. I looked in the mirror and didn't like what I saw.

I said to my reflection, "Something has to change."

WHAT WILL IT TAKE?

*I didn't know where the road would
lead, but I was ready to get started.*

Sometimes we accept the current situation because it doesn't seem bad enough to take on the work of making a change. How bad do things have to get before making that change? This is one of my biggest struggles, and I know I'm not alone. Have you ever stayed too long in a job, relationship, or circumstance because it was easier to live with the current situation than it was to contemplate doing something different?

Nothing happens until you **Commit to Change.** Change looks scary. Sometimes the path seems too steep. We too often settle for less because the devil we know is less intimidating than the devil we don't, and we only change when we run out of choices and are given no other alternatives. To move forward, we have to accept what it will take to change and make things different. To make them better.

You don't have to hit rock bottom to turn things around. Many people have made major life changes when they had no alternatives left, but you don't have to run out of choices to change direction. If you are dissatisfied with your current situation, you may not be able to fix it in one day, but you can at least take action to prevent it from getting worse.

You don't have to fix everything. You did not get where you are overnight, and you won't get where you want to go overnight, either. Change takes time, and lasting change takes effort. That's the bad news. The good news is that you can always make things better.

Do one thing. Then do the next thing. Choose one thing to change. Focus on it, and work on it. When that gets better, you'll find you can accomplish more, and other things in your life can improve as well.

Start from where you are and go from there. If you get started today and do something, I know it can lead to all sorts of wonderful and amazing changes. When I left the hospital, I could walk to the mailbox. When I got on the scale in November 2012, I was disappointed in what it said, but that was where I had to start.

I knew the road ahead was going to be difficult, but at least I had made the decision that I didn't want to stay where I was. I didn't know where the road would lead, but I was ready to get started.

I wanted to change.

PART FOUR

GET OUT THE DOOR!

22

DAVID, KILLER OF FITBITS

I started to consciously, and later subconsciously make better choices.

In November 2012, I was at the end of my patience. That morning of November 22, Thanksgiving Day, when I tipped the scales at 250.5 pounds, I knew nobody held me down and forced food on me—I had done this to myself. I knew I had to deal with my eating issues; I had to stop using food to stifle my anger and emotions.

I knew if I starved myself or went on some trendy diet, I'd lose weight, but how many times have you seen someone lose weight quickly, then bounce back to a higher weight than when they started? I realized if I was going to be successful, I'd have to do this slowly and steadily.

Around this time, fitness trackers started to become popular. I bought my first Fitbit and promptly lost it. I got another one and kept better track of it until it went through the washing machine. I got a third one. In later years, when people speak of me, I'll be known as "David, Killer of Fitbits." I lost, broke, or replaced seven Fitbits over a four-year period. It was a hassle to keep replacing them but using a fitness tracker made it easier to be accountable and track my progress.

I began to log my food consumption in an application called "My Fitness Pal," which was a useful tool for logging and tracking what I ate, especially when it tracked prepared or restaurant foods. It also shared data with Fitbit.

Once I started logging food and counting my steps, it became a game to see how many steps I could walk in a day. I knew I had to eat less and exercise more, but these two applications made it easier to measure the reality of my behavior and kept me honest. The scale, wrist tracker, and applications all communicated with each other and gave me a great way to know my numbers.

Walking was easy to monitor. My fitness tracker did an excellent job of monitoring how much I walked. At the time, I worked at the Pentagon, which happens to be the world's largest office building. Instead of using the adjacent parking lot, I parked at a nearby shopping mall and walked approximately one mile to work. Once inside, I'd walk about four miles, and then another mile back to the car. I burned a lot of calories walking six miles every day.

In MyFitnessPal, there was no fudging the numbers. If I didn't stay below my target calories, I'd get a reminder. If I ate too many carbs, it would tell me. If I had too much sugar or salt, the application would highlight the excess in detail. Consciously, I started to make better choices, and later, I did it subconsciously.

CHAPTER 22

Slowly and steadily, the weight began to come off. As I got down to around two hundred pounds, I began to consider other possibilities besides walking. I loved to ride my bike, but it was hard to ride in the wintertime or rain, and I wanted some alternatives.

A few short years earlier, I wouldn't have considered the possibility, but now, as crazy as it sounded, at fifty-two years old—I wanted to run.

I was a runner in high school. I loved running cross-country as well as track. That wasn't by design. I joined the cross-country team because I hated getting hit in football. It turns out, I had a knack for it and ran throughout high school. I was never the fastest runner on the track, but I was fast enough.

At the age of twenty-nine, I ran my first marathon, which happened to be the New York Marathon. I didn't train well for it, and while I did well for the first nineteen miles, the last seven were a death slog of shin splints and cramping quads. I couldn't walk up or down stairs for a week. I had to take them facing backward.

Four years later, I ran the Marine Corps Marathon the same year Oprah Winfrey ran it. I trained smarter this time and finished around 4:20. It was not fast, but thirty minutes faster than when I ran the New York Marathon and twenty minutes faster than Oprah. Throughout the race, the Marines yelled, "Oprah's right behind you!" to get you motivated to keep running. It turns out Oprah was a couple of miles behind, but the Marines know motivation.

I missed running. I was afraid to run, but I thought, *I'll take it easy and back off if I need to.* On the first day, I went outside, started walking, and broke into a jog. I jogged sixty feet. It was the distance between two lampposts on my neighborhood street, not much more than the length of four parked cars.

When I was released from treatment for my back injury eight years earlier, I asked the doctor all the things I could or couldn't do.

"As long as you feel okay, I don't think you have any restrictions," Dr. Childs said.

"Can I run?"

"Yeah, if somebody's chasing you."

The next day, I jogged the length of two lampposts—not consecutively, but I'd jog for one section, and walk the next, then jog another section. In the first week, I just practiced those two sections. The following week, I increased it to three sections, sixty feet at a time, jogging, then walking.

It wasn't great, but I didn't feel like I had to be great. I just had to get out the door. Once I got out the door, it was a lot harder to go back in and go to bed. Some days, I felt awful when I went out, but I never felt that way when I finished. I always felt good coming back from a run, even if it was a slow one. Every week, I went a little bit farther. Before long, I'd jog-walk all the way around the block until I made it through to my first mile.

I signed up for my first 5K run.

23

5K TO HALFWAY

Over time, as my strenth improved,
I was able to run longer distances.

Over the next year, I worked to improve my eating habits. The weight slowly came off. Other people started to notice, too. When asked, I'd say, "I'm trying to get to my original weight: seven pounds, seven ounces."

But the truth was, the numbers only told part of the story. Sure, I was in better shape, and my clothes fit better, but the significant change was that I *felt good*. I was eager to get out the door in the morning and sad when I couldn't get outside. Just being outside and taking in the scenery as I walked, jogged, or rode my bike provided a new lease on life.

As I got stronger, I took on more races, not because I was fast. I was mostly a back-of-the-pack runner, but I was just happy to be out there. My first 5K was in late March, which was in cold weather, but as spring weather arrived, I had fun collecting shirts from all the races.

My daughter and I even ran a Father's Day 5K together, where we wore Batman and Robin shirts.

Nearly 9 years later, my first race since the accident.

Over time, as my strength improved, I was able to run longer distances. The 5Ks were fun enough, but I moved up to an 8K (roughly five miles). The finish was fun because it started downhill, then rose up for the last quarter mile. I felt strong enough to pass several runners on the way up. Later, I moved up to a 10K run. When that proved to be uneventful, I signed up for a ten-mile race.

The Reston 10 Miler, in Reston, Virginia, started out easy enough. A lot of runs in the area started in cold weather. I would start out in a hat and gloves, wearing multiple layers, and shed clothes as I went. The only problem was the choice between carrying my extra clothes for several miles or donating something I didn't want to carry.

In this race, I saw that the weather forecast was going to be overcast and temperatures wouldn't be too harsh during the run, so I wore what

I thought I'd finish in. The sun did not listen to the weather report. It was bright and sunny. The temperature went up accordingly. By the time I got to mile six, I was hot. By mile eight, I was dehydrated, and in the last mile, people were asking me if I was okay.

When I run, I sometimes make-believe that I'm the Terminator.

I responded that I was fine, but I was swearing under my breath. I couldn't wait to get off the course and sought out every opportunity for shade. Mercifully, I was able to finish the race, but I made a mental note to wear cheaper extra layers next time in case I had to ditch any clothes.

By October 2013, I was down to 180 pounds and signed up for the next level challenge. I entered the Indianapolis Monumental Half-Marathon. It was 13.1 miles, in my home state of Indiana. I made a post about my commitment on Facebook, so now I had peer pressure to keep me accountable as I worked toward the goal.

On November 2, 2013, I woke up in Indianapolis at 4:30 a.m., just east of the state capitol, where my sister and brother-in-law joined me for the race. I stood in the early morning chill, wearing my sacrificial sweatshirt and sweatpants, a warmer hat, and an extra pair of gloves. When the race started, I planned to ditch the outer layer at the start and shed gear as temperatures dictated and modesty allowed.

Once the sun came up, I pulled out my sunglasses and ran on. I felt pretty good, and it was a friendly and supportive crowd. If you had a logo on your shirt or hat, people would shout those names in encouragement. Bands played on the side of the road, and there was plenty of water and energy stops with first-aid check-ins every few miles.

Any race you start, you're already a champion.

Fortunately, I didn't need any first-aid, and the course was flat, for which I was thankful. I made sure to get some water at every stop and slow down to walk or stretch when I needed it. As I reached the halfway point at 6.5 miles, the course split in two, with the full marathon runners heading off into the distance.

I turned onto the next part of the half-marathon course, one step in front of the other. My iPod Shuffle was clipped to the back of my hat, and my running rhythm changed with the song. Some songs were faster; some were slower. When Bruce Springsteen's "Born to Run" came on, I surged ahead and caught my breath during slower songs.

At each water station, I slowed down to a walk to make sure I could drink without coughing, choking, or tripping. Once I cleared the station and threw away my cup of water or Gatorade, I'd start walking faster and ease back into my pace. No longer just jogging, I ran.

As I wound through the Indianapolis neighborhoods, I thought about how far I'd come, and that I was actually having fun. The accident was nine years behind me. I was surprised I thought about it at all.

I rounded a turn onto Meridian Street and headed south toward Monument Circle. I had made it past the ten-mile marker, and later, eleven miles. There was a little over two miles to the finish. I started to push harder, but my body started telling me, "Sorry, this is all you're going to get today." I slowed my pace a bit, and my lungs and legs agreed this was the best decision.

Even though the course was almost entirely flat, the later blocks seemed to turn slightly uphill. I turned off Meridian onto New York Street, then onto Capitol. I started pushing harder toward the end, but I didn't get any faster; at least I was still going.

I rounded the final turn onto Washington Street and charged toward the end, only to see some other runners blast by me as they ran across the finish line. Fine. As my high school coach told me, "If they have that much energy at the end of the race, they weren't pushing hard enough."

As I ran across the finish line, I looked down at my watch: one hour, fifty-three minutes—a sub-8:40 per mile pace. I was jubilant when I realized I'd just finished a half-marathon.

If I could run a half-marathon . . . how much more can I push myself?

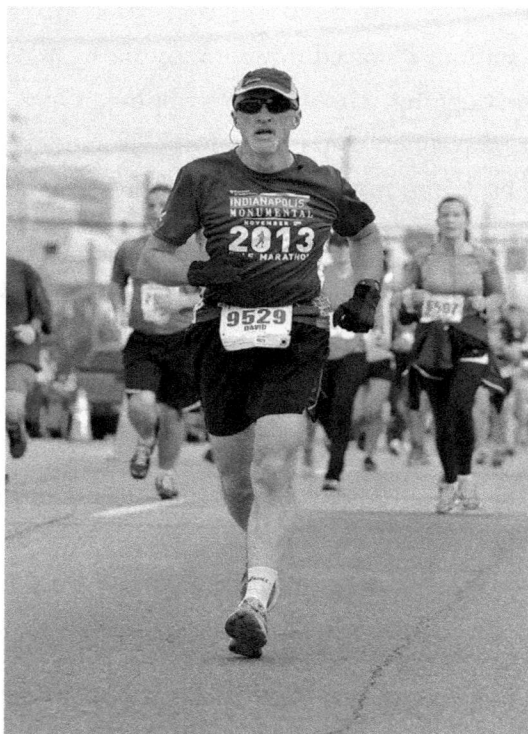

Finishing the Indianapolis Half-Marathon.

24

BUCKET LISTS

*At fifty-three years old, I
knew I'd have to train a lot.*

As 2013 ended, I considered my bucket list. I think everybody has one—things you really want to do before you "kick the bucket." For some, it's skydiving; for others, it's seeing Paris. I put together a bucket list when I was a lot younger, and looking at it, I was surprised to see what I'd already done, but several items still weren't completed.

I went skydiving when I was in my twenties. I'm glad I got that one behind me. I ran a marathon before I turned thirty, so that was taken care of as well. I had "learn to ride a motorcycle" on my list, but, well, you know how that turned out.

After I completed the Indianapolis Monumental Half-Marathon, I wanted to run and complete another full marathon. I finished the New York Marathon in 1989 and the Marine Corps Marathon in 1994. Twenty years after the first time I ran it, I added the 2014 Marine

Corps Marathon for the following October to my list because I wanted to get back to where I was before the accident. At fifty-three years old, I knew I'd have to train a lot, but I felt confident from the recent half-marathon. I wondered, *What else should I put on my list?*

I'd never tried a triathlon. I added a Sprint Triathlon to my list. It's the shortest version, so I figured it wouldn't take too much effort; I'd only have to swim 750 meters, and the bike/run portions were pretty short. If I could keep from drowning in those 750 meters, I was confident I could finish the bike and run parts of the race. I put off thinking about how to get in and out of a wetsuit since that seemed more difficult than the actual event.

It bothered me that I hadn't finished the 2008 Assault on Mt. Mitchell. That ride was originally on my list after reading about it in *Bicycling* magazine while I was in college. It was one of the few things from my college bucket list I hadn't yet completed. I'd trained poorly for my 2008 attempt and was in better shape this go-round. There was a six-month gap between the 2014 ride and the Marine Corps Marathon, so I added that back to my list. It would give me something to do besides run all the time, and cross-training would help keep me from getting injured.

I made the mistake of discussing bucket lists on a LinkedIn forum. The group discussed athletic events and bucket lists. I read through the usual "run a marathon" posts, the more ambitious "complete an Ironman triathlon," and the initial "get off the couch and do a 5K" posts. I'd recently seen a video of a building stair-climb event, so I jokingly posted, "I'd like to run up the Empire State Building."

A little while later, I got a private message from Alicia Windroth O'Neill, the corporate events director for the Multiple Myeloma

Research Foundation (MMRF). I was already familiar with the MMRF because a high school friend had been diagnosed with the disease, and I'd contributed to some fundraising events on his behalf. We messaged back and forth.

"David, do you still want to run up the Empire State Building?" Alicia asked.

"I was kind of joking, Alicia, when I posted that, but sure, I'd like to try it."

"I'd like for you to join our team that's going to be running a fundraising event for this cause."

"Sure; what do I have to do?"

"If you raise $2,500 for charity, you will be guaranteed a spot in the Empire State Building Run-Up in February 2014."

"That's no small feat—I've been reading up on the event. I know only five hundred runners are allowed because the stairways are not that wide—and they make more money on tourism than they do leases, so shutting it down for two hours once a year is significant. I'll definitely give it a go."

"Great. I will sign you up. Just so you know, if you don't raise the money, it's okay because it will still be a healthy tax-deductible donation to the MMRF."

Even though I knew it would make a considerable dent in my bank account if I did not raise the funds, I felt confident enough to sign up for the event. The year 2014 was ten years after my 2004 accident, so I could justify that it was technically an anniversary to celebrate. In many ways, it was my tenth birthday since learning to walk again.

With an air of trepidation and hesitancy, I started to map out how 2014 was going to look on paper:

In February, I'd participate in a local indoor rowing competition.

Two days later, I'd travel to New York City for the Empire State Building Run-Up.

2014 BUCKET LIST
☐ CRASH-B Sprints Rowing Competition
☐ Empire State Building Run-Up
☐ Assault on Mt. Mitchell
☐ Peasantman Triathlon
☐ Black Bear Triathlon
☐ Marine Corps Marathon

In May, I'd go back to Spartanburg, South Carolina, for a second attempt to complete the Assault on Mt. Mitchell bike ride. Also, in May, I'd attempt my first (Sprint!) triathlon.

In June, I'd scheduled a second Sprint Triathlon, just in case I didn't make the first one. That gave me about four more months to be ready for the Marine Corps Marathon. All I needed to do was keep up my current running fitness, not get injured, do all these other events, *and* double my longest-running distance from 13.1 to 26.2 miles in four months.

Bucket list, indeed. I'd be lucky if I didn't kick the bucket.

All I had to do was just keep getting out the door.

After that, the rest was going to be easy—I hoped.

ROW, ROW, ROW

I parked my car and walked into a
whole universe dedicated to rowing.

For my first bucket list item, I signed up for the CRASH-B ERG Sprints, to be held on February 2 in Alexandria, Virginia. Now, you may wonder just what the heck are the Charles River All-Star Has-Beens (CRASH)-B ERG Sprints? ERG is short for rowing ergometer, specifically, a Concept2 (C2) rowing machine. I have no idea what happened to Concept1 (C1), but the C2 rowing machine is pretty much the best way to row without actually getting wet.

At one point, a group of Olympic and world-class rower "has-beens" used to compete with Harvard's rowing team. They won a lot of races despite never practicing or using the same lineup twice. As Concept2 rowers got to be more widely used, the regional competitions came to be known as CRASH-B Sprints.

In my rehabilitation, I used a Concept2 to build strength in my legs. Since I hadn't done much rowing since then, I decided to sign up for the shortest race, a 2,000-meter sprint. I logged all my rowing in the Concept2 database and even got listed in the world ranking for my age group. Now, I was listed near the bottom of the group, but it was fun to have my name in the books.

I did several workouts to build up my rowing ability—slower, longer workouts; interval workouts; and some where I pushed as hard as I could until my lungs gave out. I even found an used, inexpensive Concept2 rower and was able to refurbish it with a minimum amount of maintenance. That way, I didn't have to go to the gym; I could go down to the basement, throw a movie in the DVD player, and practice.

The days when I didn't run due to cold weather, snow, or general soreness, I'd get on the rowing machine. That was a good thing because we got a few heavy snows in early 2014—not as big as "Snowmageddon" in 2010, or "Snowzilla" in 2016, but big enough that I didn't want to go outside.

On the morning of February 2, I drove to T.C. Williams High School in Alexandria, Virginia. That's the same school featured in the movie *Remember the Titans*. I parked my car and walked into a whole universe dedicated to rowing. I only rowed on a machine, so I wasn't part of the culture, but this high school was packed with people who lived and breathed rowing. I walked into the gym where the competition was to be held. The floor was filled wall-to-wall with rowing machines covering the entire gymnasium. The race was about an hour away after I completed my registration. I warmed up a bit and grabbed a bagel and juice from one of the concessions.

CHAPTER 25

I started to get a bit nervous as I looked around at all of the other competitors. I was in fair shape, but there were athletes ranging from eighteen to eighty (and even ninety!). They were all in great shape. I was thankful my race was only going to last less than ten minutes. I wanted to finish and get back into my warmup gear before somebody realized I didn't belong here.

I entered the warmup room with my age group heat. I chatted with the others and realized I was the least experienced out of any of them. Everybody was friendly and gave encouragement. That made me feel a little bit better, but I was still nervous about how the heat would turn out.

We were moved from room to room by the race organizers. They staged the different races and athletes. Occasionally, a rower who'd just finished his heat would stagger into the locker room, red-faced and gasping for air. A, I wondered, *What are they doing to these people out there?*

Lots of rowers, and not a boat in sight.

We moved from the locker room to the gym and took a seat in the bleachers while we waited for our heat to be called. In addition to the hundreds of rowing machines, you could hear high school, college, and regional teams cheering on their favorites as their team members pushed themselves to the limit.

I heard a whistle as a race organizer called our group to the front. They marched us to a line of rowing machines and set us each in front of our nemesis for the next ten minutes. I did a final stretch, prepped my watch, sat down on my machine, and positioned my feet in the stirrups. I adjusted the straps to secure my feet and moved the seat back and forth to make sure I wouldn't fall off in the middle of the event.

I put on my headphones, clipped my iPod Shuffle to my shirt, and hit play. Bruce Springsteen's "Born to Run" roared in my ears while I put my hands on the rowing machine handle and took a deep breath as I waited for the starter to give us the signal. I looked across our line of rowing machines, noting that while I may have been the weakest person there, I still showed up to compete.

At the end of our row was a big, tall guy built like Thor. When the starter said, "Go!" we all pulled back hard to get started, but when Thor pulled, the front of his rowing machine would lift off the ground with the force of his effort. It was clear I wouldn't be giving Thor any competition that day.

There are different schools of thought about how to row a fast 2,000 meters. Some favor starting out slower and increasing speed as you go. Others suggest finding a manageable pace and sticking to it. I was not in either camp. My rowing style could best be described as "fly and die." I rowed as hard as possible for as long as I could. I figured it would be over before I keeled over.

I made it through the first 1,000 meters faster than my previous practice attempts, but I was clearly getting winded. Every pull seemed harder to finish than the last, and I was starting to get a little lightheaded. Earlier, I had seen buckets near several of the rowers, and I was beginning to realize why they were there. I was hoping to finish without having to avail myself of one.

With 500 meters to go, the tunnel vision started, and I could feel my mouth getting dry. *If I could just get the last two minutes done without throwing up, I'd count it as a victory.* Two hundred more meters and I was into my final minute. I could see the rower counting down—fifty meters, thirty, twenty, ten, and done!

I let go of the handle and put my feet on the ground as I prayed for the room to stop spinning. After what seemed like half an hour but was only about two minutes, the room stabilized, and I was able to stand up, stagger to the bleachers, and guzzle a Gatorade I had in my gym bag. I could hear cheering in other parts of the gym as somebody set a record or someone else won a tightly contested race.

I was happy enough to pick up my gear and get to the car because, in two days, I had to exert myself in a different direction.

Straight up.

2014 BUCKET LIST
✔ CRASH-B Sprints Rowing Competition
☐ Empire State Building Run-Up
☐ Assault on Mt. Mitchell
☐ Peasantman Triathlon
☐ Black Bear Triathlon
☐ Marine Corps Marathon

26

TAKE THE STAIRS

*All in all, what started as a distant
'bucket list' item was now a reality.*

I was sore and tired after I finished the CRASH-B Sprints on Saturday. I took the Amtrak up to New York for the Empire State Building Run-Up. It was an exciting event, from the training and fundraising leading up to the climb to the event itself.

I had one fundraising goal: to raise $2,500 for the MMRF. That's what I needed to do to qualify for the team. Initially, I didn't set my sights higher because I'd never done fundraising before. If I had to write a check myself, I could afford it. It would hurt, but at least it was tax-deductible.

Being new to this, I chased publicity any way I could. A story was featured in the company email newsletter and one in the local *Fairfax Times*. The article was reprinted in *The Washington Post*, and even my hometown newspaper, *The Kokomo Tribune*. I posted stories on Patch.

com, my blog, and my neighborhood Nextdoor.com site. Between those outlets, Facebook, LinkedIn, and an email campaign, I was able to reach nearly eighty individual donors who nearly doubled my initial goal.

Picture from local news about the Empire State Building Run-Up.

Donations came from neighbors, newspaper readers, and friends from all around the country. I even got contributions from Germany and Australia. I was delighted with the results. They paled in comparison to the fundraising efforts of others. Several people raised over $50,000. All told, we raised close to $800,000 for the MMRF for a one-day event.

Two weeks before the Run-Up, I broke my toe in training due to all the constant pounding on stairs. I was afraid to go to the doctor since he might pull me from the event, so I Googled "how to treat a broken toe." WebMD and several friends advised me to "tape it to the next one," so that's what I did. I modified my run to more of a hike, taking two stairs at a time, and using my arms to pull me up.

The night before the Run-Up, New York City got four inches of slushy snow-mess that made walking around the city a challenge. I stepped on what I thought was pavement but happened to be a twelve-inch-deep puddle of icy water. With my feet soaking wet and rapidly turning blue, I started looking around for a store that might sell boots and socks or at least garbage bags I could put over my feet, so I didn't get frostbite.

I woke at 6:00 a.m. to meet the MMRF crew on the set of the ABC television show, *Good Morning America*. We were mostly "background," but we got our signs and jerseys on camera several times. It was exciting to be there to see Robin Roberts, George Stephanopoulos, Amy Robach, and Ginger Zee. There are a lot of moving parts you don't see on camera. The crew worked hard to make sure everything went off without a hitch.

My shoes hadn't dried out from the night before. Once we left the ABC studio, I resumed my search for dry footwear. I saw a City Sports store with a sign that said, "Winter Clearance Sale." I ran in, bought a pair of discounted Sorel boots, some dry wool socks, and new running socks, and sprinted back to the hotel to stuff my ASICS® running shoes full of newspapers and dry the insoles. It wasn't a cheap solution, but a necessary one.

The Run-Up is done in a two-hour block of time on a weeknight since that's the slowest time for tourists. Our team gathered in the Heartland Brewery on the Empire State Building's ground floor.

As the start time approached, the organizers gathered the burst wave of elite athletes for their start time. I was more concerned with staying upright than being fast, so I held back for the time trial wave. They allowed one runner to start off every five seconds.

Starting my watch before the big climb.

We saw the first wave go off, and it was our turn to step up to the line, one at a time. Finally, my turn came, and the volunteer said, "Go!" I ran to the door and started heading up. Immediately, it felt different than my training. The stair runs were longer, and the pitch was different. I was quickly pushing my heart rate way over the desired target. I had to work to calm myself down and try to settle into some semblance of a pace.

The first ten floors seemed to go by quickly, but I could tell it was going to get tough. With floors eleven through twenty, I was still going along but started to feel it. By the thirtieth floor, I felt a bit overwhelmed. I could continue to do two steps at a time, but I didn't know if I would make it at that pace. Reluctantly, I switched to one-step intervals. There was a water stop somewhere around the thirty-third floor, where I grabbed a cup and sipped for the next ten floors.

By the halfway point, on floor forty-three, I felt like I was in trouble. I was very overheated and tried to stop thinking about how much farther there was to go. Pace-wise, I was on target, but I was not sure how long I could sustain that speed. By the fiftieth floor, I had serious doubts. The next water stop was at floor sixty-two, and I needed it. I tried to only think about getting to the seventieth floor.

At seventy, I thought about pulling over for a break. I didn't want to stop because while I'd recover a bit, it would take a lot more mental energy to get going again. I kept chugging along, pulling up the railing. Something happened with my thinking around floor seventy-two. I realized there were only fourteen floors to go. I only focused only on the next floor. Suddenly, I was in the single digits. Floors eighty-four and eighty-five seemed hard, but they went by fast.

At the final destination, the eighty-sixth floor, I came out to dozens of camera flashes and cheers of supporters, race officials, and volunteers. I eventually caught my breath and got my finisher's medal. Because there is not a lot of room at the top, we were quickly shepherded to the elevator back down and got to see runners still queuing up for their turn. As we walked back into the Heartland Brewery with our medals, it was great to hear applause from total strangers.

86 floors and 1,576 steps. Time to celebrate!

All in all, what started as a distant bucket list item was now a reality. I may have climbed the stairs myself, but I had a lot of help from all the individual donors. At the time, I was one of fewer than 7,000 runners who've climbed the Empire State Building. At the same time, I got to be part of a larger cause. We raised awareness, visibility, and funds for the MMRF.

Now, when I look at what seems to be an insurmountable obstacle or an unreachable goal, I know I've got this in my back pocket as proof that I can achieve it. And whenever I walk by the Empire State Building, it doesn't look nearly as tall.

2014 BUCKET LIST
☑ CRASH-B Sprints Rowing Competition
☑ Empire State Building Run-Up
☐ Assault on Mt. Mitchell
☐ Peasantman Triathlon
☐ Black Bear Triathlon
☐ Marine Corps Marathon

27

LAST PLACE FINISH

*I was nearly in tears from the cramps
and stress of trying to keep going.*

In May 2014, I went back to Spartanburg, South Carolina, to make another attempt at the Assault on Mt. Mitchell. The 102-mile ride, with over 11,000 feet of climbing, is rated as one of the most challenging rides in the country, according to *Bicycling* magazine. It had long been a bucket list item of mine, even more so since I'd attempted the ride in 2008 and had to drop out at the eighty-seven-mile mark.

I wanted to complete the ride this time around. I felt like I had given up too early in 2008. If I trained properly and rode carefully, I could pull it off. I saw that many older riders and athletes with all sorts of physical challenges had finished, and I wanted to be part of that group.

I started training earnestly for this ride in November 2013. I booked a hotel room for the 2014 race, joined the Freewheelers of Spartanburg Cycling Club to get an early entry, and started training. Because of the protracted winter in DC, I was stuck indoors until nearly April, allowing less than two months to do any serious training. In the end, I was only able to get in three longer rides to prepare, although two of them had some steep climbs similar but not as long as Mt. Mitchell. I decided I was as in-shape as I was going to get and took the weekend before the ride to rest up.

After a long day on Saturday volunteering with the Toastmasters District 29 speech contest, I took off on Sunday morning for the seven-hour drive to Spartanburg, South Carolina. Fifty miles into the trip, my GPS failed. I spied a Walmart just off the highway. I took the exit and ran into the store to buy a new GPS unit. I hooked it up and was back on the road in less than fifteen minutes.

I arrived in Spartanburg in time to pick up my race packet and get settled. I saw two Krispy Kreme donut stores right across the street from each other. I think that might be where Starbucks got the idea. I checked into my hotel, went next door to get a big pasta meal, and came back to get ready for the next day.

6AM, and ready to start the climb.

While I didn't sleep much, I rested well before waking up at 5:00 a.m. I suited up, loaded the bike on the car, and drove to the start line. I made some small talk with other riders, and at 6:30 a.m., the Assault on Mt. Mitchell officially started. The first few miles were fast, with lots of bike traffic, close passes, and large pelotons—riders drafting one another in a group. I made good time and averaged eighteen to twenty MPH for the first segment. The first rest stop was at twenty-two miles, so I took a quick bathroom break, wolfed down some food, and climbed back in the saddle.

The next rest stop at forty-four miles was another quick off and on, and then it was on to our first big climb at Bill's Hill. It's only a mile long, but the first part was a double-digit climb. I made it to the top and enjoyed a quick descent down the other side. This was fun! We took rest stops at the sixty-five-mile mark and at seventy-three miles. This was no big deal to me now, and I felt great.

An early hill climb. I still felt good here.

After a ten-minute break at the Tom Johnson Campground, I started up NC 80 toward the Blue Ridge Parkway. The first part was easy, with beautiful views of a stream and lake on the way. Once we got to eighty miles, the grade increased, and at mile eighty-five, my quads began to cramp. This was not a good sign. I limped along toward the Blue Ridge Parkway rest stop, where I quit in 2008. Back then, I was wiped out due to one hundred-degree temperatures and dehydration, and I'd run out of time. This time, I felt a bit weak, but I wasn't going to stop in the same place.

I was about an hour ahead of the ride cutoff, so I worked out the kinks in my legs and got back on the bike. The first part of the Blue Ridge Parkway was pretty cool. It was reasonably level, and I got to ride through two tunnels. The views off to the side were spectacular. Once I got past the short downhill part and started climbing again, my legs started cramping so badly I had to get off the bike before I fell. Every time I tried to get back on, they'd seize up again. I decided to try and walk the bike for a bit so I could get my legs back.

At the ninety-mile marker, I was off more than I was on the bike. Whenever the grade would flatten out, I'd get back on, pedal for as long as I could, and walk again when the cramps returned. I still had twelve miles to go, all uphill. I began to worry that I'd run out of time. At each rest stop, I'd do some major stretching and get back on.

At the ninety-seven-mile rest stop, one of the volunteers gave some vocal encouragement to riders as they left the lot. As they rolled out, he'd yell, "Push it!" By that point, I was hurting so bad that I had to ask him not to say anything when I rolled out. He saw how much pain I was in and gave me some encouragement to get going again. That helped because I was nearly in tears from the cramps and stress of trying to finish.

At the one hundred-mile rest stop, I still had an hour to go. I thought even if I had to walk all the way, I could still make it. Prior to that, the broom wagon drivers would check in on me frequently, asking if I needed any help or if I wanted to quit. I did not want to drop out again. I asked how many riders were behind me, and the first time they said seven. Later, it was five, then two, and at one hundred miles, they told me I was the last rider on the course. That meant everybody was waiting for me to finish or quit. I soldiered on, with the green broom van following me, waiting to sweep me up. I felt like I was being stalked by the Grim Reaper.

I may have finished last, but I still won.

I made it to 102 miles. With a half-mile to go, I started to think I was going to beat the deadline. All of a sudden, I turned my foot the wrong way, both of my calf muscles seized up, and I fell. I already had one foot down, so it wasn't far, but every time I tried to move, it felt like someone was sticking a knife in the back of both of my legs.

At that point, I was in tears. A park ranger came around the corner and thought I'd been hit by a car because I was partially in the road. Fortunately, I wasn't injured, just cramped up in knots. He helped me stretch the calf muscles out to where I was able to get back on the bike.

I struggled up the last hill, and it leveled off to a parking area. As I turned the corner, the volunteers at the finish line started cheering—both of them. The clock said 11:50:32. I had barely beat the final cutoff—by ten minutes.

Most of the finishers received hot soup and food and had a chance to change their clothes. I only had time to grab the bike, receive my finisher's patch, shove my dry clothes bag in my arms, and march onto the bus. It was a hasty end to a long day. No matter how bad I felt, or how long it took, I have the distinct honor to be the last official rider to complete the 2014 Assault on Mt. Mitchell.

Of the 820 riders who started, 611 finished before me. I was number 612. So, in spite of it being a "last place" finish, I think of it as a badge of honor. No matter how bad I felt, no matter how dark my mood, I kept going. It would have been easier and much less painful to get in the truck and ride home, but I had set out to finish, and that's precisely what I did.

In reality, I won.

2014 BUCKET LIST
☑ CRASH-B Sprints Rowing Competition
☑ Empire State Building Run-Up
☑ Assault on Mt. Mitchell
☑ Peasantman Triathlon
☐ Black Bear Triathlon
☐ Marine Corps Marathon

28

TRI, TRI AGAIN

*Other than the climbs, the
ride was scenic and uneventful.*

As part of my 2014 anniversary year, I did some things that only a few years previously would have seemed impossible. The first half of the year included the indoor rowing competition, the Empire State Building Run-Up, the Toastmasters District speech contest, and, in May, the Assault on Mt. Mitchell. It was a busy year.

One of my other bucket list items was to complete a triathlon. I didn't feel the need to go all-out for a grueling Ironman event. Instead, I set a more modest goal of completing a Sprint Triathlon. That's a 750-meter swim, an eighteen-mile bike ride, and a 5K run. Sounds easy, right?

A triathlon seemed like a natural progression after all the running and biking competitions. What made it a bit harder is that you are required to do all three segments back-to-back. You have to swim in an extremely cold lake early in the morning, then ride the bike portion, and run the final leg. I had to put in a lot of swim training because I needed to improve. I was never a serious swimmer. If I got out on the other side of the pool, I considered that a success.

In January, I joined the DC Tri Club. Its New Triathlete program seemed like it was built for amateurs like me—structured enough for training and support, but flexible and affordable enough to fit my schedule. On a snowy January day, my fifty-third birthday, I sat in a DC public library meeting room with two hundred other prospective triathletes.

They explained everything and made it seem accessible and achievable, so I signed up. I also signed up for the beginner swim clinic. Fortunately, I was more of an intermediate swimmer than a true beginner, but the great instructors worked with swimmers of all levels. I slowly increased from ten laps to twenty to where I was able to swim a half-mile. A few weeks later, I swam a full mile and increased that to a mile and a half. The Tri Club put on running and biking clinics, too. Fortunately, I felt confident in my abilities in those areas, so I could practice and build up my mileage on my own.

Swimming in a pool was one thing, and swimming in cold open water is something else. One of the pieces of equipment I needed was a wetsuit. I received lots of good advice and discounts from the Tri Club. Things got real the day my new wetsuit arrived in the mail. I opened the package and thought, *How am I supposed to fit in this?* I read the instructions then started stuffing myself into the suit. I got it all the way on and tried to zip it up. I wondered if I'd gained weight. I learned it is supposed to be hard to zip up, and there's a trick to doing it. I still felt like I was stuffed in a duffle bag, but it fit.

In May, I tried my first open water clinic in Lake Anna with a water temperature of sixty-two degrees Fahrenheit. The really cool thing about a wetsuit is that once you get wet, you don't get cold. It works to keep you warm, and it floats. Despite being a bit restrictive on my stroke, I could float effortlessly in the suit, and it made my first practice triathlon much less of a scary thing. The next day, I "competed" in the Peasantman sprint triathlon. This particular triathlon wasn't a competitive race, but it included a swim, a bike, and a run, so I felt I could finish a real one.

This seemed challenging but easy in comparison to the Assault on Mt. Mitchell. With my preparation complete, I rested and prepared for the real thing. All I had left was to drive four hours to Northern Pennsylvania.

I hope these numbers aren't permanent.

Until I signed up for this event, I never knew there was an actual town called Jim Thorpe, Pennsylvania. It's a neat little place, and the town was welcoming to the large crowd of prospective triathletes who crowded into the local Italian restaurant for the pre-race spaghetti dinner. After getting a full load of carbohydrates, it was off to bed to get some sleep before the 5:00 a.m. wakeup.

I think I slept. I must have because I remember parts of some dreams, and I also remember turning over a lot because my mind was racing well before post time. The alarm went off, and I got up, dressed, grabbed some food, and hauled all my equipment down to the car. At the start, I got my race number marked on my arm and my age on the back of my leg. I was wondering if they were also going to post dental records in case I didn't make it through the race.

The calm before the start.

About half an hour before the start, I squeezed into my wetsuit and walked down to the beach. One of the entrants said that the water was a "balmy" sixty-four degrees. I put my foot into the water. It was frigid. That didn't stop some athletes from swimming without a wetsuit. I was glad I had mine. I got used to it once the sensation of cold water pouring into the suit subsided. I did warmup exercises in preparation for the start. This was a "swimming" start, which meant we swam out to the middle of the lake and treaded water until the horn went off. That made for less jostling and bumping at the start, although I swam over a couple of people, and a few bumped into me. While visibility was a bit of an issue, I followed the swimmers in front of me, and twenty minutes later, I ran out of the lake to my first transition.

Triathlon swimming involves swimming, breathing, and avoiding kicks to the head.

I peeled off my wetsuit, put on bike shoes, gloves, helmet, and glasses, and pedaled off to the bike route. According to one person, there were 900 feet of climbing on the course. I thought it would be a piece of cake. It was a hilly ride, with at least ten hills over a 10 percent grade, with a couple topping out at 16 percent. More than a few riders had to get off and walk their bikes up the hills. I was lucky to have my triple crankset with a low granny gear, which made climbs tough but still achievable.

Other than the climbs, the ride was scenic and uneventful. I arrived for transition number two. I racked the bike, flipped off my bike shoes, slipped on my running shoes, and swapped the helmet for a hat. I was off for the run. On my practice triathlon, I had a tough time switching to running and had to walk a lot. This time, I felt slow, but I could actually run. We had a lot of shade, not too many hills, and a beautiful view running over the dam and looking out toward the mountains. Mile one went by, then two, then back to the lake for mile three, and I turned the corner for the finish. I heard my name on the PA and saw my daughter, Lauren, at the finish line. I was done!

The drive home is the nicest part of the race.

That was another bucket list item checked off. With all the other events checked off, it was time to get serious and get ready for the Marine Corps Marathon.

2014 BUCKET LIST
☑ CRASH-B Sprints Rowing Competition
☑ Empire State Building Run-Up
☑ Assault on Mt. Mitchell
☑ Peasantman Triathlon
☑ Black Bear Triathlon
☐ Marine Corps Marathon

29

SEMPER FI!

*Each week, I'd do a longer
and longer run on Saturdays.*

As I recovered from my motorcycle accident, it took six months to get cleared to go back to work and a full year before I was released from treatment. I spent the next year learning to get back to "normal," which also included getting back into cycling since the doctor had suggested I stick to nonimpact activities when I could.

What struck me most was the huge effect my recovery had on my family and my job during the full year it took to get released from treatment. I decided I was tired of my current situation and needed to do something different.

Over time, I built up my running distance, making sure I gave myself enough room for rest and recovery. The hardest part wasn't running— it was getting off the couch and in motion. Once I got out the door, it was easier to keep going than it was to go back inside, so I made it a point, no matter what, to get moving.

With 2014 marking ten years since my accident and twenty years since my last marathon, I decided to take on the Marine Corps Marathon. I qualified by running the Marine Corps 17.75K run in April 2014, which included about eleven hilly miles. I put together a training program to build up to the full distance. The speed runs and cross-training were straightforward. The long runs? Well, they were—long.

Each week, I'd do a longer and longer run on Saturday. I was good up until I got over fifteen miles and found I was running out of gas. I made sure I was drinking and refueling during the runs. Eating while running isn't easy, but there are all sorts of products that, while not exactly real food, will give you enough energy to keep running. That allowed me to move up to eighteen, then twenty, and peak at the longest run of twenty-two miles. Before my long runs, I'd set beach towels on the recliner and put my iPad and television remote on the table next to it. Because after the run, that's where I'd be for the next two hours.

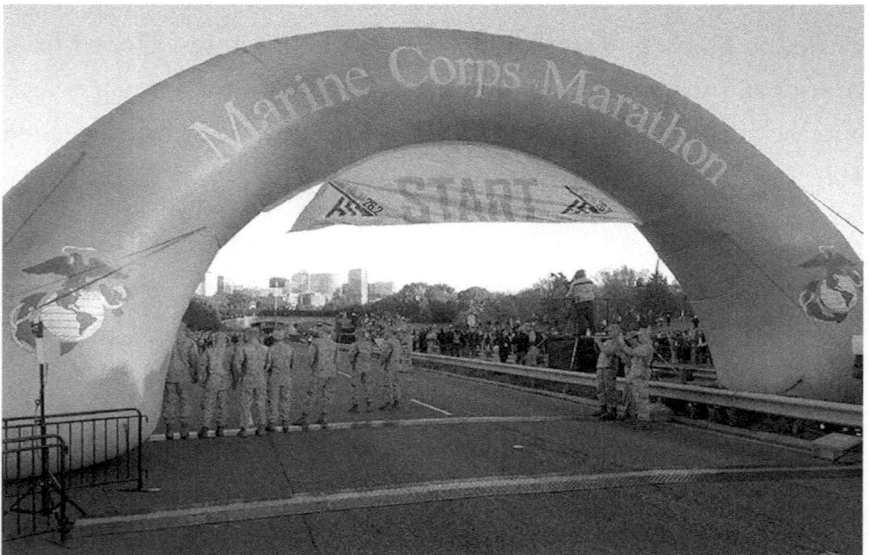

Nearly 40,000 runners at the start of the
Marine Corps Marathon.

Since I'd been blogging about my recovery and had run in a couple of races sponsored by the Spinal Research Foundation, my story gained some interest in the local area. Comcast SportsNet came out to interview me and featured my interview on its Marine Corps Marathon news segment. I also got invited to a pre-race event where I got to meet Medal of Honor recipient Kyle Carpenter and actor Sean Astin.

The race has a lot of nice scenery.

When race day finally arrived, I got up at 4:00 a.m. and drove to the Pentagon. I waited in my car for a few minutes in the parking lot. I walked in the dark to the staging area for the start of the race. I got to see Carpenter skydive into the start of the race, surrounded by other skydivers carrying the American flag. I watched several V-22 Ospreys fly overhead, right before the cannon fired, signaling the start of the race.

For the first 10K, I ran faster than I'd expected and felt great. At the seventeen-mile mark, I started to have a bit of stomach trouble. I slowed significantly by mile nineteen. Despite drinking at every water stop, I felt dehydrated, something I attributed to the warmer-than-expected afternoon. There were no clouds in the sky, and the pavement was warm, too. By mile twenty-one, I had to slow to a walk. I was dry-mouthed and shaky. More than once, I thought about sitting down and calling it a day.

Around 17 miles, I'm starting to slow down.

I slogged through the next four miles, and at mile twenty-five, I picked back up to a slow jog. I knew if I kept going, it would be over soon. Not long after that, I could see the turn going up the hill toward the Marine Corps War Memorial. Once I turned, I kept chugging away, hearing the crowd cheer and the Marines giving encouragement to everyone staggering toward the finish. I crossed the line and couldn't believe it was over. As I walked toward the bag pickup and on toward the Metro to ride home, I hear, "Daddy!"

My daughter, Lauren, had been following my progress on Facebook and arrived at the finish just in time to meet up with me. Despite feeling shaky, it made my day a lot brighter. I ran a lot slower than expected for the last ten miles, but I finished. I was disappointed in the time, but I only had to think back a bit to realize—

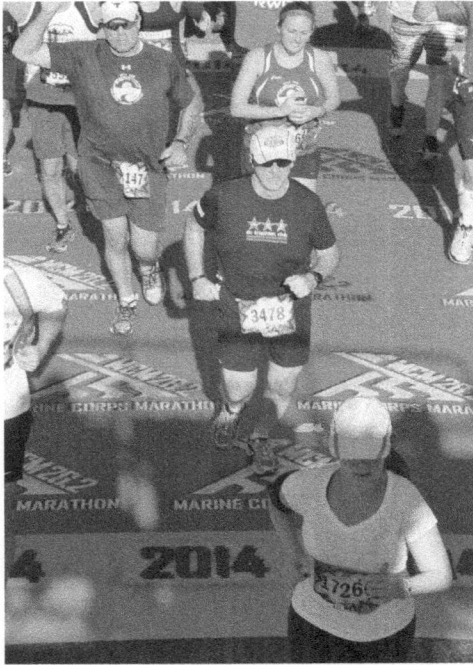

Every step is once step closer to the finish line.

Ten years earlier, I didn't know if I would walk again.

Two years earlier, I weighed 250 pounds.

Twenty months earlier, I jogged sixty feet.

And that day, I ran a marathon.

I looked back over the past decade and found it hard to believe how much had changed. I also considered that, while I had some goals I wanted to accomplish, I never created elaborate plans or programs to go after them. The most important thing I learned was that any big plans mattered less than getting out of bed and on my way. The most important thing was to—

Get out the door! After that, the rest was easy.

2014 BUCKET LIST
✔ CRASH-B Sprints Rowing Competition
✔ Empire State Building Run-Up
✔ Assault on Mt. Mitchell
✔ Peasantman Triathlon
✔ Black Bear Triathlon
✔ Marine Corps Marathon

30

SCHOOL OF HARD KNOCKS

I wasn't always happy with the results,
but I was thrilled with any progress.

I never learned things the easy way. When I was a kid, I was stubborn (and I still am). I'm not good about taking advice, listening to smarter people, or being methodical about getting from Point A to Point B. If I want to do something, I usually jump in and start doing it (badly).

Speaker Zig Ziglar said that "anything worth doing is worth doing poorly until you can learn to do it well." I tend to live by that maxim. When I started playing the guitar, I played it poorly, but kept at it, until I either drove away all my listeners or got good enough to have some of them come back. When someone compliments my talent, I'm grateful and thank them, but add they're lucky they didn't have to hear all the work it took to become talented.

In college, I worked at a resort north of Chicago, where I had the good fortune to work with some Second City improv actors who taught me how to do sketch and stand-up comedy. I was bad at first, but over time, I got a little better each time I was on stage. I learned that what you see on television and on stage is the finished product. You rarely get to see all the hard work, bad mistakes, and poor performances that led to that moment.

That's been true for everything I've done in life. I've had some lucky breaks from time to time, but a lot of my good fortune has just been from getting up and getting out the door to try again. When I was first married, we bought a house that took both our incomes to afford. We'd moved down from Connecticut, and I commuted into Arlington, Virginia, every day. The job wasn't exactly what I thought it would be, and within six months, I got fired. I was terminated on the day of the company Christmas party.

At first, I was in a panic. I'd never been fired from a job before; I worried if I'd ever find another job and whether we'd lose the house. Fortunately, I was able to line up another job after the first of the year, and we kept the house. We also got our first dog, Scout, who was with us for the next eleven years. Even when things looked bad, if I got back up and got going again, everything seemed to work out.

When I joined the Toastmasters organization, I wanted to learn how to speak better in public. My first few speeches were bad, but I tried to learn from each one. I even entered its speech contests, and in my first contest, I lost—at the first level. It was frustrating, but I got up and tried again, winning at the club, area, and division level, then losing at the district levels. I never placed at the district level until my fourth attempt, where I finished second. Two years later, I finally won at district and went to the semifinals at the international convention in Chicago. Out of 35,000 speakers who started, I was in the final hundred or so. When it came to my turn, I did a good job, but I went overtime and was disqualified.

Sometimes, that's what happens. You get up, and you take a swing and miss. You get up again and miss. You get up a third time and barely get further than you did the previous time. I found if I viewed things as a win or lose situation, I always came away disappointed. When I started trying to be a little better, every situation became a win/win situation. I wasn't always happy with the results, but I was thrilled with any progress at all.

That's how I learned to walk again—not by doing any one thing but by doing lots of little things and getting help from lots of people. If I was willing to try, so were they. If I asked for help, I frequently got it. I had to admit I wasn't perfect, ask for and accept help, and then work my butt off to make progress, no matter how little that progress was, or even if it wasn't in a straight line. I had to pay attention to what was going on around me and take advantage of the opportunities when they occurred.

There's an old story about a farmer who had a mule who wouldn't pull a plow. A traveling salesman said, "For twenty dollars, I'll guarantee I can make him pull that plow."

The farmer agreed and gave the salesman the twenty dollars. No sooner than he handed it over, the salesman took a two-by-four and whacked the mule right over the head.

The farmer shouted, "Why in the world would you do that?"

"When you want somebody to do something, first, you must get their attention," replied the salesman.

In 2004, the motorcycle accident got my attention. My entire life was disrupted, and I had no choice about my hospitalization. Once I was forced to pay attention, I had to make choices about what I wanted and where I wanted to go.

In 2012, I was reminded of where I wanted to go, and that I had to change to get there. It wasn't going to be easy, but if I got up and kept getting out the door, I could make progress.

Sometimes you have to be hit over the head, but wouldn't it be better to learn from someone else's mistakes? That's what I'm trying to inspire you to do. I'm trying to show you what mistakes I've made, share what I've learned, and help you avoid some of the pitfalls. Maybe the lessons will be easier to learn.

Now that I have your attention.

THE ROAD AHEAD

*From time to time, I've had to adjust
and refocus when I've gone off-track.*

It's been an interesting time since 2014. I've gone through a lot of changes, a lot of ups and downs, and like everyone else, I've put a few more miles on my odometer and tried to learn a thing or two. As I pointed out earlier, progress is rarely in a straight line. Sometimes, things go in a different direction than what I'd like, but the road continues to stretch ahead, and I try to keep moving forward.

There have been several setbacks and bumps in the road where I've had to adjust my direction or speed. In 2009, my company merged with another, and I had to not only find a new job but also reinvest in my technical education and certifications to make sure I kept current with industry trends and remained employable.

In 2015, I changed jobs again because the company I worked for was going through a shift in focus. The funny thing was after I left to work for my current company, in 2018, it acquired my previous employer, and I ended up working with a lot of my former co-workers again. That reminded me that you should always be positive and professional.

The same year, Maggie and I went through a year-long divorce that had been coming for some time. Divorce is never easy, and it's rarely one-sided. I knew I needed to take ownership of my part and move forward. My main concern was that the kids would be in a good place and have a decent relationship with each parent, and I could let go of the past. While I've worked hard to make sure my relationship with the kids is strong, and they're both moving forward as young adults, making peace with my mistakes is not easy. I'm still working on that.

From time to time, I've had to adjust and refocus when I've gone off track. My weight has gone up and down, and as I get older, it gets harder to take the weight off. That makes me no different than anyone else in my age group. Knowing that gives me some comfort, but my goal is to stay healthy and active for as long as I can. To do that, I need to keep making more good choices and fewer bad ones.

I've set other goals that I've added to my bucket list. After completing the Marine Corps Marathon, and later, the full Indianapolis Monumental Marathon, I set my sights on the Disney Marathon. It's the same 26.2 miles, but the course runs through all the Disney parks in central Florida. My daughter and I ran the Princess 10K and half-marathon, and the following year, I targeted the Dopey Challenge. It consists of four races, on four consecutive days: a 5K, a 10K, a half-marathon, and finally, the full 26.2 miles. Each day, you run twice as far as the previous day, for a total of nearly fifty miles.

I trained for a full year to make the race. When I got there, the 5K and 10K were no big deal, but during the half-marathon, I started to develop IT band issues, causing a stabbing pain in my thigh. I'd spray a freezing agent on my leg that allowed me to run farther, but at the end of the half-marathon, my daughter Lauren reminded me that starting a marathon when I was already injured might be a good way to make an injury permanent. Reluctantly, I listened and went to the doctor when I got home.

At first, I thought I was having hip and IT band issues. That much was true, but there was a different cause than what I previously thought. After laying off from running for over a year, I went to the doctor because my hip pain persisted. The x-ray showed that my hips and knees were fine, but there was an issue in my spine. Between the fusion surgery, my age, the stress above and below the hardware, and my 2008 accident, I'd had some deterioration in the space between my L4 and L5 vertebrae.

Even though I've had great results from my spinal fusion, fifteen years post-surgery, I'm not as young as I used to be. There is some narrowing between my L4 and L5 vertebrae, which is causing pain and weakness on my left side. According to the doctor, I may need another surgery at some point, but for now, we're treating it with cortisone injections and physical therapy. I'm optimistic, but I also need to be realistic about how to best take care of myself over the long term. I'd rather be walking and not running than not walking at all. I keep moving forward.

I'm excited about creating new goals and experiences. I've been working on my speaking and writing skills and learning how to tell my story in a way that's beneficial for the audience. If my story helps someone who's going through a similar challenge or struggling with a difficult situation, that's a greater reward than any speaking trophy or race medal.

As I mentioned before, as I made my journey through rehabilitation, I joined Toastmasters to learn how to speak better. That's been useful in building my skills and confidence in front of a group. Through all the competitions and contests, I learned that most people in a contest don't win. If you're only focused on winning, you'll likely be disappointed. I frequently think about Mark Brown's 1995 Toastmasters World Champion's statement, "Your life tells a story—and there's someone out there who needs to hear it." That's what I'm trying to do—learning how to tell my story in a way that helps those who need to hear it.

Sometimes, I get off track. In the year after my leg injury, I let my weight creep up due to lower activity and stress eating. It's hard to get on the scale and realize I'm not exactly where I want to be—but I also know if I keep doing the right things, I'll start moving in the right direction and get back on track.

The road to where I want to go is never a straight line. It has hills and valleys, twists and turns, and sometimes a big detour sign. However, if I keep going, I will get there.

I just have to get out the door! After that, the rest is easy.

32

WHAT ABOUT YOU?

My journey continues. It's not always
in a straight line, but it is mine.

When I got on that motorcycle on July 9, 2004, I had no idea how my life might change, what I would learn, and how far I would go in the ensuing years. It's been an incredible journey, with more twists and turns than I could have ever imagined. It is an incredible story, and it happens to be true. Time and distance may have clouded a memory or two, but the internet doesn't forget. It was easier than I thought it would be to dig up old blog entries and find old pictures or newspaper articles to document the journey.

This can be your story, as well. When I first started thinking about putting this together in a book, I thought it would be hard for people to identify with the story or find any similarities with my struggle. What I discovered was that everybody has struggles and challenges in their life. While our individual challenges may differ, we all have places we want to go. We all have obstacles thrown in our way, and we all find ourselves frustrated with what life puts in front of us.

When I first started speaking in Toastmasters contests, I told stories I thought were funny or entertaining, and I advanced in the contests as I got better. After not placing in my third district contest, a friend came up and said, "I love your stories, but you've got to stop talking about you."

I was confused for a time, but I eventually got what he said. When I thought about it at length, what I think he meant was, I had to stop making me the focus of the story. I may be the main character, but if I focus on the accomplishment, people find it hard to identify with a hero who doesn't make mistakes.

Instead, I've focused on the struggle and mistakes. The victories are sweet, but without the effort, pain, and challenge, they don't mean much. Life doesn't give participation trophies. Every achievement brings bumps, bruises, and scars that may fade with time, but stick with us as reminders of what it cost to get this far.

My ten-inch scar, two titanium rods, and four screws are reminders of what it cost to get to where I am today. If I don't take care of myself and stay ahead of any symptoms, I'll be even more aware of the cost. While it takes a lot of effort to keep moving forward, staying in place costs even more.

My journey has been a long one. Over the past fifteen years, I've gone places I never thought I could go, but it doesn't end here. My journey continues. It's not always a straight line, but it is mine.

CHAPTER 32

I believe while our journeys may not be identical, they have a lot of parallels. We all struggle with setbacks and self-doubt. My challenge to you is:

What about you?

What do you want to do?

Where do you want to go?

You don't have to be great, spectacular, or even average. I think most of us start out as ordinary. If we stay static and don't try, that's all we'll ever be. If we try and fail, it might be embarrassing. It might hurt. But then again, you might learn something. If you learn something, anything, from the attempt, it's a win. That's how you move from ordinary to extraordinary.

I don't think there's a point in life where you can sit down and say, "I'm done. I've achieved everything I wanted to achieve." That's why I think most lottery winners end up bankrupt and miserable. They mistake money for satisfaction. Don't get me wrong. I've had money, and I've needed money, and having it helps you do things that money can buy.

What I've found is the value of what money can't buy. Money won't give you any more time or friendships. It may make the struggle easier, but true happiness comes from the struggle. Knowing you've accomplished something yourself can make all the hard work worthwhile.

33

GET OUT THE DOOR!

The Longest Journey begins with a single step.

It's been a long journey from 2004 to now, which brings me back to where I started. My journey may be unique to me, but I believe that our stories are similar. We all want to go places that we've never been to. We all want to achieve things when others may doubt our ability or commitment. We all run into obstacles or setbacks that make us wonder if the goal is worth it.

As I said at the start of this book, the path to your goals is rarely a straight line. It's full of obstacles, naysayers, left turns, and self-doubt. It's hard to stay focused on the big goal when everyday life keeps throwing little things at you that try and knock you off-balance. No matter how consistent you are about writing down goals, throwing yourself into your work, executing plans flawlessly, or leveraging others' experience, sometimes life has other plans that will get in your way.

Whether you're fast or slow, stay in the race.

There is only one thing I've found that will make a difference in whether you make progress or stay in place. It's not a secret, but most people avoid it like the plague, waiting for the ideal formula, perfect timing, or obvious opportunity—things that don't exist in real life. The secret is that there's no magic potion, knight in shining armor, or cavalry riding over the hill to save the day. Success is rarely thrust upon you, and never happens without a decision to act or first step into the unknown.

If there are any lessons to be learned in all this, I've tried to write this as openly and frankly as possible, and maybe, just maybe, this story may speak to you and help you to overcome an obstacle that's been standing in your way, or start moving toward a goal you've always wanted.

Remember:

To move forward, you have to **Identify the Obstacle.**

- Life has no guarantees.
- Your life can change in an instant.
- We need other people.
- Once you identify the obstacle, the path becomes much clearer.

There may be events that are beyond our control, but there is a way forward. Find those people who can help you on your journey, and you'll discover that you're helping them, too.

What a difference 1 year makes.

The longest journey **Starts with a Single Step.**

- You don't have to know the end of the journey to start.
- You may not be strong, but you can get stronger.
- Direction is more important than location.
- Start with a single step, and you can get there.

You can go to some amazing and incredible places, but you've got to get started. Once you take that first step, who knows where it can lead?

Nothing happens until you **Commit to Change.**

- You don't have to hit rock bottom to turn things around.
- You don't have to fix everything.
- Do one thing. Then do the next thing.
- Start where you are and go from there.

If you just get started today and do something, it can lead to all sorts of wonderful and amazing changes.

When I started running again, I ran all of sixty feet. That set me on a journey that has collected a lot of trophies and medals, but the internal rewards have been much more significant. It's a cliché to say the journey is more important than the destination, but without the journey, the struggle, and the changes you go through along the way, the destination has no meaning or value.

There is one thing you can do to make your life better tomorrow than it is today. There is one thing you can do consistently to achieve your goals and go where you want to go. All you must do is—

Get Out the Door! Once you do, the rest is easy.

Get out the door! The rest is easy.

ACKNOWLEDGMENTS

This book would not have been possible without the help and support of many people who gave me encouragement throughout the process. First and foremost, I'd like to thank my family, without whose support there would have been no book to write. Thank you to my sister, Jennifer Slack, who helped get me through the early days of my recovery and continued to inspire me throughout the journey. Thanks to my big sister, Pam Surack, who was never shy about giving me a push when I needed to get moving.

I am grateful to Ronald Childs, MD, and the team at Inova Fair Oaks, Inova Mount Vernon, and the PT team at OrthoVirginia for their superior medical care that gave me the ability to turn what seemed like an ending to the beginning of something great.

I want to thank Judy Carter for her inspiration to turn my story into something that can inspire others. Thanks to my long-time friend, David Goad, for his coaching, feedback, and encouragement to get this story written down. Thanks to Cathy Oasheim for her editing skill and tenacity in helping me shape the events into a coherent story, and also to Henry DeVries and the team at Indie Books International for their help in turning the text into a finished product. I couldn't have reached this point without the effort of many people, for which I am forever grateful.

ABOUT THE AUTHOR

David Hollingsworth is an award-winning speaker, author, and storyteller who has performed at The Moth, DC Improv, and Stand-Up New York. He was also a semi-finalist in Toastmasters' World Championship of Public Speaking. In his professional career, David has more than twenty-five years of experience as an information technology professional in the corporate and federal worlds. David earned his MBA from Xavier University and graduated from Ball State University in Muncie, Indiana. David lives with his family in the Washington, DC, area. He has completed more than ten one hundred-mile bicycle rides, four marathons, three triathlons, and too many 5Ks to count. To contact David about speaking or bulk orders of this book, email him at david@holliworks.com.

EVENT LIST

EVENT	LOCATION	URL
Army 10-Miler	Washington, DC	https://www.armytenmiler.com
Assault on Mt. Mitchell	Mt. Mitchell, NC	https://theassaults.com
Back Roads Century	Shepherdstown, WV	https://www.potomacpedalers.org/back-roads-century
Black Bear Triathlon	Jim Thorpe, PA	https://www.cgiracing.com
Cherry Blossom 10-Miler	Washington, DC	http://www.cherryblossom.org
Disney Marathon Weekend	Lake Buena Vista, FL	https://www.rundisney.com
Disney Princess 10K and Half-Marathon	Lake Buena Vista, FL	https://www.rundisney.com
Dulles Airport 5K	Dulles, VA	https://potomac.enmotive.com
Empire State Building Run-Up	New York, NY	https://www.esbnyc.com/event/empire-state-building-run-up-info
Gallop and Gorge 8K	Carrboro, NC	https://www.cardinaltrackclub.com
Indianapolis Monumental Half-Marathon	Indianapolis, IN	https://monumentalmarathon.com
Marine Corps 17.75K	Prince William Forest Park, VA	https://www.marinemarathon.com/events/17-75k
Marine Corps Marathon	Washington, DC	https://www.marinemarathon.com/events/marathon
Mid-Atlantic ERG Sprints	Alexandria, VA	https://www.ergsprints.com
New Year's Eve 4 Miler	Fairfax, VA	https://www.runpacers.com/race/fairfax-four-miler

New Years' Day 5K	Reston, VA	http://www.prraces.com/newyearsday
Peasantman Sprint Triathlon	Lake Anna, VA	http://www.highcloud.org/peasantman
Ragnar Relay DC	Washington, DC	https://www.runragnar.com
Reston 10 Miler	Reston, VA	http://www.prraces.com/perfect10
Run for Haiti 5K	Reston, VA	http://www.prraces.com
Run with Dad Father's Day 5K	Reston, VA	http://www.prraces.com/runwithdad
Seagull Century	Salisbury, MD	https://seagullcentury.org
South Lakes 10K	Reston, VA	http://www.prraces.com/southlakes
We've Got Your Back 5K	Reston, VA	https://spinehealth.org

ORGANIZATIONS/ LOCATIONS

Blue Ridge Parkway
Asheville, NC
https://www.blueridgeparkway.org

City Sports
New York, NY
https://www.citysports.com

Concept2 Rowing
Morrisville, VT
https://www.concept2.com

DC Tri Club
Washington, DC
https://www.dctriclub.org

Freewheelers of Spartanburg
Spartanburg, SC
https://freewheelers.info

Good Morning America
New York, NY
https://www.goodmorningamerica.com

Inova Fair Oaks Hospital
Fairfax, VA
https://www.inova.org/locations/inova-fair-oaks-hospital

Inova Hospital System
Fairfax, VA
https://www.inova.org

Inova Mount Vernon Hospital
Alexandria, VA
https://www.inova.org/locations/inova-mount-vernon-hospital

Mount Mitchell State Park
Burnsville, NC
https://www.ncparks.gov/mount-mitchell-state-park/home

Multiple Myeloma Research Foundation
Norwalk, CT
https://themmrf.org

New York Road Runners Club
New York, NY
https://www.nyrr.org

OrthoVirginia
Fairfax, VA
https://www.orthovirginia.com

Potomac Pedalers
Washington, DC
https://www.potomacpedalers.org

Potomac River Running
Ashburn, VA
https://www.potomacriverrunning.com

Spinal Research Foundation
Reston, VA
https://spinehealth.org

SHARE YOUR STORY!

I hope this book has been inspiring for you. I'd love to hear your stories as well. If you would like to share your story of getting out the door, send it to stories@holliworks.com.

SPEAKING AND CONFERENCES

I'd love to speak to your group or at your conference and inspire your audience to get started on their next big adventure. If you are interested, contact me at speaking@holliworks.com.

BULK ORDERS

Get Out the Door! is available on Amazon.com in both physical and eBook versions. If you or your organization would like to purchase books in bulk or gift orders, send your request to sales@holliworks.com.

FOLLOW ME ON SOCIAL MEDIA!

Several of the stories in *Get Out the Door!* were originally published on my blog at www.holliworks.com. If you'd like to engage with me on social media, we can connect at:

H www.holliworks.com

@holliworks

@holliworks

www.facebook.com/holliworks

www.linkedin.com/in/holliworks

APPENDIX
PHOTO CREDITS

Page #	Photo Credit
9	Photo courtesy of David Hollingsworth (2004)
21	Photo courtesy of David Hollingsworth (2004)
23	Image provided by David Hollingsworth (2004)
25	Image provided by David Hollingsworth
90	Photo courtesy of David Hollingsworth (2008)
91	Article courtesy of *Fairfax County Times* (June 25, 2008)
92	Photo courtesy of David Hollingsworth (2008)
112	Photo courtesy of PR Races (2013)
113	Photo courtesy of PR Races (2013)
114	Photo courtesy of PR Races (2013)
116	Photo courtesy of MarathonFoto (2013)
123	Photo courtesy of David Hollingsworth (2014)
128	Photo courtesy of *Fairfax County Times* (2014)
130	Photo courtesy of New York Road Runners (2014)
132	Photo courtesy of New York Road Runners (2014)
136	Photo courtesy of David Hollingsworth (2014)
137	Photo courtesy of Joe Shrader Photography LLC (2014)

139 Photo courtesy of Joe Shrader Photography LLC (2014)

145 Photo courtesy of David Hollingsworth (2014)

146 Photo courtesy of David Hollingsworth (2014)

147 Photo courtesy of David Hollingsworth (2014)

148 Photo courtesy of David Hollingsworth (2014)

152 Photo courtesy of David Hollingsworth (2014)

153 Photo courtesy of MarathonFoto (2014)

154 Photo courtesy of MarathonFoto (2014)

155 Photo courtesy of MarathonFoto (2014)

170 Photo courtesy of David Hollingsworth (2014)

171 Photo courtesy of MarathonFoto (2012, 2013)

173 Photo courtesy of David Hollingsworth (2014)

www.ingramcontent.com/pod-product-compliance
Lightning Source LLC
Chambersburg PA
CBHW031931190326
41519CB00007B/488